STREAMS

MURRAY ANDREW PURA

STREAMS

REFLECTIONS *on the* WATERS *in* SCRIPTURE

ZONDERVAN®

ZONDERVAN.com/
AUTHORTRACKER
follow your favorite authors

ZONDERVAN

Streams
Copyright © 2010 by Murray Andrew Pura

This title is also available as a Zondervan ebook. Visit www.zondervan.com/ebooks.

This title is also available in a Zondervan audio edition. Visit www.zondervan.fm.

Requests for information should be addressed to:

Zondervan, *Grand Rapids, Michigan 49530*

Library of Congress Cataloging-in-Publication Data

Pura, Murray, 1954–
    Streams: reflections on the waters in Scripture / Murray Andrew Pura.
      p.   cm.
    Includes bibliographical references.
    ISBN 978-0-310-31838-5
    1. Water in the Bible. 2. Water — Religious aspects — Christianity I. Title.
BS680.W26P87 2009
    220.8'5537 — dc22   2009032589

All Scripture quotations, unless otherwise indicated, are taken from the Holy Bible, *New International Version*®, *NIV*®. Copyright © 1973, 1978, 1984 by Biblica, Inc.™ Used by permission of Zondervan. All rights reserved worldwide.

Scripture quotations marked TNIV are taken from the Holy Bible, *Today's New International Version*™, *TNIV*®. Copyright © 2001, 2005 by Biblica, Inc.™ Used by permission of Zondervan. All rights reserved worldwide.

Scripture quotations marked MSG are taken from *The Message*. Copyright © 1993, 1994, 1995, 1996, 2000, 2001, 2002. Used by permission of NavPress Publishing Group.

Any Internet addresses (websites, blogs, etc.) and telephone numbers printed in this book are offered as a resource. They are not intended in any way to be or imply an endorsement by Zondervan, nor does Zondervan vouch for the content of these sites and numbers for the life of this book.

Cover design: Studio Gearbox
Cover photo: Veer
Interior design: Michelle Espinoza

Printed in the United States of America

---

10 11 12 13 14 15 • 23 22 21 20 19 18 17 16 15 14 13 12 11 10 9 8 7 6 5 4 3 2 1

for John of the Rivers

Contents

Foreword

by Eugene Peterson

The revelation of God — who God is and what God does — is given to us in the form of story. Not propositions of truth, not commands and rules, not definitions and explanations, not prohibitions and promises. None of that. *Story.* It is important to know this so we can receive and respond to the revelation on God's terms, not on our terms. The revelation of God is story shaped; our lives are story shaped.

The Devil and his angels are employed full-time in effacing and distorting — *de*storying (destroying) this storied revelation. The strategy is to fragment the story into bits and pieces and get us to arrange the pieces however we like to make ourselves better or get ahead in the world or patch up our bruised and broken lives with splint and Band-Aids and do-it-yourself potions. The Devil doesn't bother with denying or sowing doubts on the truth of God as it is revealed in the Bible. He just wants to get rid of the story, the story that insists that creation and salvation take place in bodies, in the company of men and women, in families and neighborhoods, in communities where babies are born, children play, and eventually everyone dies. His strategy is to cut up all the verses in the Bible and hand them over to us to arrange however we like, picking out our favorites and dealing into the discard pile the ones we don't like or have no interest in. Jesus and other men and women in the biblical story end up as flat paper-doll figures that we are free to dress up any way we fancy and then use them to play religion.

Fortunate for us, there are a considerable number of men and women who energetically and skillfully are at work countering the diabolical strategy by reassembling the truths and commands, the promises and prohibitions, into stories. A lot of them are Christians. They make sure we understand the biblical revelation as a story of fully alive — feet-on-ground, flesh-and-blood, body-and-soul — men and women. And they make sure we understand ourselves as storied people whose lives have plot, character, and purpose. They do everything they can, and they can do a lot, to keep everything we think and do, love and hope and believe, *personal*, *relational*, *local*. Nothing abstract, nothing disembodied, nothing disconnected from life in the neighborhood.

Murray Pura is among our best storytellers on the Christian front. In *Streams*, he tells five biblical stories — using rivers, oceans, and lakes as metaphors — in which all the action and presence of God is revealed in actual geography and weather, people and circumstances. Next to these biblical stories he juxtaposes contemporary stories — his and ours — in which God is revealed among us in our lived humanity. As the stories come into proximity with one another, we begin to notice God revealed in our stories. These stories — the Bible stories along with our stories — are not written to entertain or "teach us a lesson." They pull us into the world of God's presence and action as participants. We don't watch the action as spectators; we *become* the action.

Asked by one of his friends why he told stories, Jesus said he told them "to create readiness, to nudge the people toward receptive insight" (Matthew 13:13 *The Message*). *Streams* are stories told in this Jesus tradition.

Eugene Peterson, professor emeritus
of spiritual theology, Regent College,
Vancouver, BC, Canada,
and translator of *The Message*

We never know the worth of water till the well is dry.

Thomas Fuller, *Gnomologia*, 1732

THE PATH TO WATER

It always happens.

Pick up a game trail in the forest, and eventually it will take you to water. Lost in trees and brush and rock by the sea and not sure how to find the beach? Get on any path, and one way or another it will make its way to the ocean. How to make it to a creek or river or stream? Find a path, even the most narrow, and step by step it will take you to the place where birds and deer and fox find their evening drink.

We took a path that wound down to the river. Not just any river. This was the mighty Fraser in British Columbia, Canada, and we weren't sure what to expect, but we definitely wanted adventure. Two canoes. Two of us in each. For hours we didn't need to paddle as we moved south and west with the current. The bows hissed. We laid back and enjoyed the scenery.

We knew there were rapids somewhere ahead; we just didn't know what it would look like when we hit them. The moment suddenly came, and the hair rose on the back of my neck—whirlpools, waves, and whitewater. "Paddle!" my companion urged. I dipped and dug as though my life depended on it. I remember the eye of that whirlpool gazing at me as we were swept into its constrictions—the eye had no life and no kindness. I strained with the strength that rises with adrenaline and fear. We chopped our way through the white swirls and snapping waves. Spit out on the other side, we saw our friends waiting for us in calmer waters and raised our paddles over our heads and gave two mighty roars of triumph.

A few hours later, we came around a bend in the river and saw not hundreds but thousands of Canada geese resting in gray, brown, white, and black splendor. It was autumn, and they were taking a break before heading further south. They let us paddle right among them without a honk or squawk or flapping of wings. It was amazing. Something out of some kind of heaven, a blessing that filled our hearts and delighted our eyes and turned us into four-year-olds again for ten or fifteen minutes. Our canoes glided quietly among them as we gazed in wonder. Then they heard a sound and rose swiftly as one. The air roared in our ears, and the sun vanished.

We paddled on until the sun dipped low, and we began to look for a spot to beach. Soon a large sandbar came into view, and we took our canoes there. We built a small fire, and our Bowie knives cut meat that we cooked on short sticks. There were apples and oranges and plenty of cold water to drink. The river slipped past, and soon the stars were caught up in the current and heading south too. Our tents were pitched and our bags spread. We watched the river night until the rhythms of a holy creation rocked us to sleep.

As I look back on it now, this canoe trip seems like both a God journey and the journey of a life. Companionship and the fast flow of youth. Danger and hazard overcome by hope and faith and strength. The geese representing a blessing we could not give ourselves. The loveliness of the land we moved through — and sometimes the harshness. Food and drink and the whisper of water in our ears. The river bearing us away to heaven as we slept. All from following the path to water.

There are many such paths in the Bible. The world begins with God hovering over the waters of creation and ends with the river of the water of life, as clear as crystal, flowing from the throne of God and the Lamb. Water creates the world a second time at the flood. The wells of Abraham, Isaac, and Jacob sustain their families and tribes and livestock and also God's promise of a Savior. The Nile bears Moses to Pharaoh's palace and later, by the hand of God, turns to blood, one of the miracles meant to set the people of Moses free. The Red Sea parts for Israel; the Jordan (the same Jordan that will baptize the promised Savior thousands of years later) parts for a new Israel — and they enter the Promised Land. Noah is thrown into the sea and swallowed by a great fish. Jesus walks on water and sails in boats that crisscross the Sea of Galilee. Three thousand are baptized at Pentecost. Paul is shipwrecked three times and spends a day and a night on the open ocean before being rescued. John is exiled to Patmos in the Aegean Sea.

There are many water stories, and all the stories tell us something about God and something about ourselves. It would take many books, or one big fat one, to explore each of them. So we take a few and learn from them: the Red Sea, the rivers of Babylon, the streams that speed through the desert in the rainy season, the Jordan River, the Sea of Galilee. Enough to make a good start.

My trip down the Fraser made me think of earlier days in

our world when much of the travel was done on various boats. In North America, the native people used canoes long before there was European settlement. Yet even in the days of the pioneers and the first great towns and cities, boats and barges and steamers were the means for moving people and goods from one place to another. In the region in which I was born, you can still spot old landing stages on the riverbanks where boats docked to unload passengers and cargo. How different it must have been to travel by water instead of by road, to travel on something that flowed and that moved you rather than on something that was rigid, fixed, and unyielding and that you yourself had to move on. "Rivers," wrote Blaise Pascal, "are roads which move, and which carry us whither we desire to go."*

I found the Fraser canoe trip, except for the rapids, to be smooth and liquid and freeing in a way pavement and asphalt are not. I watched people and houses and forests and fields slip past slowly, not as a blur, but as moments I could savor. In the same way, I think, traveling through the Bible by water provides a different perspective—and an important one. We see the lives of people such as Moses, Joshua, Jesus, and Peter in a unique way that often gets lost amid the details that occupy us as we look at all the land stories.

We also see our God and our own lives in that same unique way, for the Bible stories and the truths that emerge from them are a part of the great river of God that has flowed from the beginning of creation until now—and we are on that river too. We understand many of the experiences of people we read about

---

* Blaise Pascal, *Pensees* (Sioux Falls, S.Dak.: NuVision Publications, 2007), 11.

in Exodus and Joshua and Mark and Acts because we have experiences that are similar. We cry out to God in the same way and are afraid of the storms in our lives. Yet we also learn to trust God in the same way and to get out of our boats and walk on the waters with Jesus, even if the wind and waves terrify us. The stories encourage us and renew our faith because we face the same sorts of challenges with the same God and Savior at our side and in our souls.

The sons of Korah wrote a song in which they stated, "There is a river whose streams make glad the city of God" (Psalm 46:4). God is that river, and he flows right through the hearts of those who believe. And his desire is to bring fullness of life and fullness of joy. That is what this book is about. It is God's story, and it is also ours.

PART ONE

THE RED SEA
The WATERS of CHALLENGE

*So God led the people around
by the desert road toward the Red Sea.*
Exodus 13:18

ONE

"Hold on to the tiller and don't let go!"

"It's kicking like a team of wild horses!"

"Keep your grip! Don't let up for a second or we'll be on the rocks!"

"How," I asked myself, wind and water slashing my face and eyes, knuckles bone white from gripping the wooden tiller, "did I wind up in this mess, Lord?"

I had longed to see the ocean ever since I was a boy growing up on the Great Plains. In time, God would take me to more of the world's oceans than I had imagined possible. But at first it was enough to see — and touch — the Pacific and the Atlantic. Seaweed, barnacles a crust over rocks, the sting of saltwater in the air I breathed, gulls splitting the wind with their wings and their cries, and best of all waves — waves lapping and waves crashing, waves as gray as iron or as blue as the sky or as green as trees, foam as thick as snow, spray like drops of rain. Who could not love the sea in all its moods and colors and sounds? Nathaniel Hawthorne wrote, "A greeting and a homage to the Sea! I descend over its margin, and dip my hand into the wave that meets me, and bathe my brow. That far-resounding roar is Ocean's voice of welcome. His salt breath brings a blessing along with it."*

---

* Nathaniel Hawthorne, *Twice-Told Tales* (Charleston, S.C.: BiblioLife, 2008), 360–61.

It was on the broad blue and majestic Pacific that I learned to sail when I was twenty-two. Now here I was, on a thirty-five-foot boat, trying to steer into a fast tide, rocks like claws on either side, a storm up and tearing clouds into shreds over my head. My brother-in-law was just beside me, banging away at the engine with a hammer to keep it going. All sails were up. If we kept the engine at full throttle and the wind didn't drop, we thought we had a knot or two on the tide and could make it through this pass between two islands. If the wind dropped or the engine stopped or I steered off course and the tide turned the bow, we were finished. The rocks would snag the boat, rip up the hull, knock us about pretty good, and then help us drown.

It had been a shortcut. Rather than go around the islands, we decided to head between them. Too bad the current wasn't running with us. Again and again the power of the sea tried to yank the tiller from my hands. I riveted my eyes on a marker buoy I'd spotted miles ahead and tried to keep our bow locked on to it. My brother-in-law dealt the engine another blow, and there was a spurt of greasy black smoke. It coughed and rattled. My sister popped her head up from below, where she'd been cleaning up the breakfast dishes. Oblivious to the drama that was unfolding, she glanced around and then pointed, calling in an excited voice, "There's three ducks!"

My brother-in-law and I were tense as we looked forward, our eyes straining, and tried to gauge whether we were making any headway at all. For the longest time it was touch-and-go. I was sure we were being pushed back. Again and again it felt like furious horses were rearing up and smashing their hooves into our rudder. The wood in my hands quivered and shook and heaved. My brother-in-law did not consider himself a believer, but I did, so I prayed—for any extra bit of strength God could lend to my hands and arms, any extra puff of wind, any slight slackening of the tide. And soon we began gaining on the roaring tide.

"We've got her!" hollered my Belfast brother-in-law. He smacked a meaty fist into the engine. "We've got her!"

So we did. In another fifteen minutes we were in the open sea. The sky had peeled back to blue. The engine was off, and the wind was in our sails, taking us to harbor and restaurant, hot food and dry clothes. My brother-in-law grinned, the gap between his two front teeth prominent but not unattractive. "The sea opened up for us," he announced.

"He that will learn to pray," the pastor and poet George Herbert wrote, "let him go to sea."*

---

* George Herbert, *The Works of George Herbert in Prose and Verse* (London: William Pickering, 1853), 298.

TWO

Scholars argue over which sea the Israelites passed through or which part of the sea. I am not going to get into all that. The point is, they crossed through a body of water that was deep enough to drown them, yet they went over safe and dry — that's why it was a miracle. They couldn't have done it on their own. They had no means of engineering their escape from Pharaoh's troops. They were desperate for a way out. But, humanly speaking, there was no way out.

The Red Sea was a challenge — not to see how resourceful the people of God were and what sort of plan they could come up with in a moment of danger; it was a challenge to see if they had faith that God would intervene when it looked as though nothing or no one could save them. It is a challenge many of us have faced and will likely face again. And it's not an easy challenge to take on, regardless of how deeply committed to Christ we are.

What happened in the sailing boat was frightening, and things could have gone from bad to worse. I believe prayer made a difference. But what I experienced was a small thing compared to the challenges others look in the face — cancer, murder, financial ruin, mental illness, divorce. They need God to part the waters for them in a big way, and often enough there is very little others can do for them or they can do for themselves.

We know Israel's story.

Slaves in Egypt. Set free by a series of divine miracles. Led by God into the desert. A pillar of cloud by day and a pillar of fire by night. Moses, Aaron, Miriam, the Ten Commandments, the golden calf, the Promised Land flowing with milk and honey.

We know the story well.

What we may not know as well are all the little details of the crossing of the Red Sea.

- After the Israelites left Egypt in haste, God took them the long way around, by the Red Sea, using the desert road. He was afraid they might lose their will to move forward into freedom if they had to fight the Philistines (Exodus 13:17–18).

- Nevertheless, Israel was armed to the teeth and ready to fight their own battles when they emerged from Egypt and left the Nile River behind them (13:18).

- Israel was safely camped at Etham on the verge of the desert country. God had them turn back. They made another camp by the Red Sea opposite Baal Zephon. He did this in order to set up a final confrontation with Pharaoh. He wanted the Egyptians to think Israel had lost its way and was trapped by the desert sands that surrounded them. His intention was that Egypt would finally grasp who he was—the LORD, Yahweh, the one true God of heaven and earth (14:1–4).

- As God had planned, Egyptian troops caught up to Israel at Baal Zephon. There was nowhere to run, God had made sure of that. Israel's faith and courage evaporated like drops of water in the desert air. They screamed at Moses, "Was it because there were no graves in Egypt that you brought us to the desert to die?" (14:11). Fear made them wish they could return to the Nile—enslaved but alive was far more appealing to them at the moment than freedom and death: "It would have been better for us to serve the Egyptians than to die in the desert!" (14:12).

- Moses told them not to give in to their fear but to have faith: "Stand firm and you will see the deliverance the Lord will bring you today.... The Lord will fight for you; you need only to be still" (14:13–14).

- God responds testily to the people's wailing (the way Jesus would often react after a score of miracles still hadn't increased his disciples' faith)—"Why are you crying out to me?" (14:15)—and tells Israel to move forward toward the Red Sea. Moses is to raise his staff over the waters so that they divide and the people can walk through on dry land (14:15–16).

- Israel's faith had been tested as Egyptian soldiers approached, kicking up clouds of dust, and the people didn't do so well. Now their faith will be tested again. The Red Sea, undivided, is at their feet and night is descending. Nothing has happened. The former slaves watch and wait, the warriors of Israel facing toward the Egyptian army. Unseen by them, the angel of God moves from in front of Israel and goes in back of them. The pillar of cloud does the same, except this they can't help but notice.

It brings light to them and darkness to the Egyptians (14:19–20).

- Moses stretches his hand over the water. All night, an east wind blows and pushes the sea back. It becomes dry land, and Israel starts walking over. Throughout the night they come by the thousands. Children, women, men—no doubt astonished, bewildered, a bit frightened and awed—are now safe on the other side, grateful. The pillar of fire and cloud gleams over them. They are in the presence of God. Perhaps they are amazed to see where a scrap of faith and obedience has taken them (14:21–22).

- The Egyptians surge forward after Israel and enter the path through the sea. Israel sees them come—we are not told how they feel. As they look, just before dawn, God throws the Egyptian forces into chaos. And Moses stretches his hand over the water so that the sea returns to normal, waves crashing together where once there was a road in the middle of the water. At sunrise, it looks like nothing out of the ordinary ever took place at this spot. But Israel is assembled on the far side of the Red Sea. The Egyptian troops are dead on the shore. The people are free. And a song begins to echo out over the desert: "The Lord is my strength and my defense; he has become my salvation" (14:23–31; 15:2).

If we want to talk about faith as small as a mustard seed, that's Israel, that's the people of God in this story. Despite the incredible things they had seen God do on their behalf in Egypt, they were sure that following God had brought them into the worst mess of their lives. In fact, they felt that having faith in God had brought them to the end of their lives. Yet what looked like the darkest moment they had ever known soon became the brightest moment.

It may have looked like a worst-case scenario to Israel, but God had planned it all along. Everything was meant to fit: the place where Israel was camped, the Egyptian troops moving in, the Red Sea an impassable obstacle at Israel's back, no allies to turn to, nowhere to hide.

God was meant to be Israel's only hope.

At first, the people did not believe that truth. They were sure they were finished. They did not believe God could rescue them from the hard fist of a world empire. But whatever tiny amount of faith they had, they used. When the sea parted, they began to walk, though some of them must have felt the walls of water might come crashing in on them at any moment. Sometimes, when God acts, it can seem too good to be true, and for a number of God's ancient people, it must have seemed as though they were walking in a dream.

THREE

We cannot be too hard on Israel because their story is often our story. God has done marvelous things in our past. But the weeks and months and years go by, and our experiences of God's acts become memories—good memories, but still things that happened long ago. When new challenges come our way, the kind we cannot see our way through, God might be viewed simply as our last resort. Or if we do come to him early, we might come skeptically and with a feeling of hopelessness that leaves us already defeated in our spirits.

Maybe we haven't felt close to God for some time and don't believe we deserve his help. Maybe there are some things we haven't addressed in our lives—struggles with forgiveness, dishonesty, violence—and we are certain we don't have God's ear anyway. Maybe we've been hurt that God hasn't answered some of our prayers the way we'd hoped, and we've come to think he doesn't really love us much. Or maybe some of us have reached a point where faith in God and commitment to his ways and his words have become real issues.

There may be a thousand reasons our faith in a God who acted dynamically in our past has faltered. Yet, as it was for Israel, it is possible for us to find just enough faith to make a big difference in the present.

When I read the story of the Red Sea, I think of the story of Lazarus in John 11.

Jesus came on the scene too late. Lazarus was already dead. Yes, his sisters had seen Jesus do marvelous things in their lives and in the lives of others. But that was last week, last month, last year. This was now. The man they believed Jesus could have healed was in the grave. It was over.

Yet, as in the event at the Red Sea, and in the Christmas story of a baby born in a manger far from his mother's home, God had a hand in how everything came together. Jesus deliberately waited for Lazarus to die: "When he heard that Lazarus was sick, he stayed where he was two more days" (John 11:6). There was a plan — though it involved pain for Martha and Mary; for Lazarus, who had to die; and even for Jesus, who would weep. "Lazarus is dead," Jesus told his disciples, "and for your sake I am glad I was not there, so that you may believe" (11:14). The plan, like the plan at the Red Sea, was to bring more faith into the world.

And more revelation of the glory of God. The two are closely intertwined, like roses enmeshed in a trellis or great cedars rooted in the earth. In Exodus, the Lord keeps saying, "Look, I'm going to do this wonderful thing for you, and you're going to see the glory of God" (see Exodus 14:17–18). God's people did see, and they put their faith in God (Exodus 14:31). In John's gospel, Jesus tells Lazarus's sister Martha, "Did I not tell you that if you believed, you would see the glory of God?" (John 11:40). Mary and Martha did see — Lazarus rose from the dead — and they put their faith in Jesus, God with us.

Mary and Martha had no idea what was going to happen. They hadn't completely given up hope, but they'd come awfully close: "Lord," says Mary, "if you had been here, my brother would not have died" (John 11:32). "Lord," says Martha, "by this time there is a bad odor, for he has been there four days" (11:39). And their friends: "Could not he who opened the eyes of the blind man have kept this man from dying?" (11:37).

They didn't see what good rolling away the gravestone was going to do, except make everyone feel even more wretched from the stench of death, but they used the little bit of faith they had. The children of Israel started walking; the friends of Mary and Martha started moving the stone. The sea parted for them both—the Red Sea for Israel, the black sea of death for Mary and Martha. Something happened that was beyond what they could ask or imagine.

These were not great heroes of the faith who saw the Red Sea open up or death conquered as Lazarus came back to life at Christ's command. They were people like us—people with many doubts and fears. Yet what little they had—and for some it was very little indeed—they gave to God. The water could have rolled in and drowned them. The smell from the grave could have made them sick to their stomachs and sick to their souls. But they took on the challenge anyway. And they saw the glory of God.

FOUR

The next morning, a Wednesday, we were leaving for Denver in our Jeep. It was late April. The weather in our neck of the woods was good, and I wanted to get an idea of the projected road conditions for our route south through Montana and Wyoming. I clicked on the TV and started looking for a weather report that would cover the rest of the week.

The first images I saw were confusing. The words *BREAKING NEWS* were spread across the bottom of the screen. The TV showed images of what looked like a school building, with students running out of it in a single line, coming across the lawn with their hands behind their heads. The screen also read, Littleton, Colorado (a suburb of Denver). I turned up the volume and found that there had been a school shooting.

Within a few minutes, I was on the phone to the church in Denver that had invited me to speak. Did they still want me to come?

"Do you know what's going on down here?" asked the secretary.

"I do. It's terrible. That's why I'm thinking we should cancel. Obviously this isn't a good time."

She told me she'd speak with the pastors. I remembered her from an earlier visit to this church in the fall, a very pleasant woman. I spoke with my wife. We prayed. We waited. And we watched the news unfold minute by painful minute.

My return to Denver had been set in January. They were expecting my wife and me, our four-year-old daughter, and our six-year-old son. A hotel room had been booked. I was supposed to do readings from my books, bring a message or two, and be prepared to interact in a small group setting. Now it was April 20, and we had planned to head out at noon on the twenty-first. Who could have had any idea in January that the worst high school shooting in United States history would occur on the outskirts of Denver in Jefferson County the very week we were supposed to arrive?

The secretary called back. The pastors wanted me to come. This had all been arranged months before the shooting, hadn't it? They felt that God wanted me here, that it was a divine appointment. I felt inadequate, but I said yes. My wife agreed. The next day, we pulled out of our driveway under clear skies and headed for Colorado.

By Thursday, we were in eastern Montana. The skies had lowered, and a cold rain was falling. We reached the Little Bighorn area and decided to stop—even at the age of six Micah had already read a lot about the history of the American West. No other visitors were around, only staff members, who told us to ignore the warnings about rattlesnakes that were posted all over the battlefield—the snakes were only active in the warm weather. We spent an hour there.

The dreary weather, so different from June 25, 1876, together with the lifeless brown grasses, the markers where soldiers and natives fell, and the iron reality of the modern-day killings we were driving toward, combined to give my wife and me a feeling of dread. Suddenly it wasn't history, but real Sioux and Cheyenne slain, real troopers stripped and dead. When we toured the museum inside the main lodge and saw the hatchets and stone clubs and rifles of June 25, I felt sick to my stomach. It was all too real. There was nothing glorious or romantic about the battle or any of the decades of warfare among the tribes and the army and the settlers. Killing was killing, and the shootings at Columbine High School put the Little Bighorn into grim perspective.

Back in the Jeep the rain turned into snowflakes. A Wyoming blizzard was underway. After white-knuckling it for several hours I noticed that the only other vehicles on the highway were semis. Snow and ice were blasting down out of the Bighorn Mountains. Our plan had been to get to Cheyenne by nightfall; I pulled off the road in Casper, grateful to be in one piece.

On the television in our motel room, we saw the weather forecast for Wyoming. A sudden storm had roared in out of the west. Snow was expected to cover Route 25, swooping in from the Wind River Range, the Granite Mountains, the Owl Creek Mountains, the Laramie Mountains, you name it. I looked at our children laughing and playing together and at my young wife, and I felt anger surge through me — *God, why did you bring us into this storm? How could you put my family in this kind of danger?* I had plenty of fury for myself as well — *Why didn't you get on a plane? Why did you put your family at risk? Who cares about this divine appointment? Do you really believe God cares if you're in Denver or not?*

So, when push came to shove, I was like Israel in front of the Red Sea: *Weren't there enough graves up north? Did you have to bring us to Wyoming to die?* I knew in my heart I was not going to drive into the sort of blizzard they were predicting. My all-season tires had been slipping and sliding enough just getting us to Casper. I shook my head. *No, Lord, no matter what is expected of me in Colorado, or what I expected of myself, I'm not budging from this motel room until the storm passes.*

The weatherman was still spreading doom and gloom, and my wife was helping the kids with supper, when I dropped to my knees by one of the two beds. This was not something I normally did. I believed, and with good reason, that God hears you whether you're sitting or standing, lying flat on your back or flat on your stomach. Prayer is a matter of the heart. But here I was, elbows on the bed, hands clasped to my forehead, eyes closed, knees on the carpet.

Lord, I'd like to be able to say I'll get in the Jeep in the morning, no matter what the weather is like, and trust you to get us through, but there's no way that's going to happen. I'm not going to kill my son and daughter and wife just to get to Denver. I don't know what's going on. I don't know why this storm blew up out of nowhere, but I just can't go any further. If you want us in Denver, you're going to have to stop the storm. You're going to have to open up the road. And I guess that's what I'm praying for. That you keep the snow in the mountains and off the highway, that you clear the road and get us to Denver, that you do what you want to do in us and through us in Colorado. I know it's a bad time there. Maybe they need all the help they can get. But this thing is too big for me.

It's in your hands. I believe you want us in Denver, but you've got to change the forecast. Lord, you've got to hold the snow back.

And that was that. I felt better for having prayed, and I'd be lying if I didn't say I felt a spark of hope where before I'd only felt anger. But I was no poster child for a life of faith. I still grumbled about the whole situation to my wife and said we'd only know what to do when we looked out the window in the morning. Maybe this was as far as God wanted us to go. Maybe he wanted us to have some quality family time in Wyoming. We talked about my going on ahead alone, but in the end decided we'd stick together, no matter what we chose to do. And eventually I fell asleep, still praying, still anxious, still wondering what things would look like at dawn. I had faith about the span of one small snowflake out of the Medicine Bow Mountains.

When I woke up, the sky was gray. I turned on the TV, and it looked to me like the same weatherman was still standing there, the large map of Wyoming at his back. The kids were stirring, my wife yawning. I had the volume on low. "The storm has not materialized," the man was saying. "The snow has remained up in the mountain ranges for the time being." I was astounded. Maybe one small part of me said, "I knew it," but most of me was staggered. The snow had remained in the mountains and had not swept down to the highway?

It was Friday morning, April 23, 1999. We had breakfast in the Jeep as we raced south. The sky was overcast, but the highway was dry and free of ice, the best road conditions we'd had in two days. The Lord opened up a path in the middle of the sea, and we took it. I can't explain what happened any other way than by saying he worked it so the roads of southern Wyoming were clear. They shouldn't have been, according to what the satellite images had shown the weathercasters. But we got into Colorado without seeing a drop of rain or a streak of sleet.

Denver was under heavy gray clouds. Snow was on the ground, and more was expected. The whole city seemed smothered by a thick blanket of grief. We checked into our hotel, and I noticed adults wearing buttons with pictures of some of the slain children on them.

The days were a mix of emotion. It was great to see the pastors and their families again, great to introduce them to my wife and children, great to pray with them and talk with them. But at the back of everyone's minds were the killings. And back of that, in my mind, was the thought, "What am I going to say on Sunday morning? What can I possibly say?"

Al Gore, who was vice president at the time, was in Denver because of the shooting. So were Michael W. Smith and Amy Grant and many others I can't recall now. On Saturday night, as the children slept and my wife and I watched TV programs about Columbine, I prayed and read passages from the Bible, continually asking, *Lord, what am I going to say tomorrow morning?* The pastors had told me that relatives of at least one of the slain would be at the church on Sunday. *What could I say to them that would make a difference?* I scribbled a few notes on a small pad of hotel stationery—no more than five or six words. We turned off the lights, and I lay praying and wrestling in the dark.

I had given messages under hard circumstances before. When a pastor friend had been shot dead years before, I had written a simple eulogy that I handed out to others but never read out loud. A mother in one of my churches lost her son in a motorcycle accident two months before his graduation from high school; his whole class was at the funeral, weeping. A man came up after that wrenching good-bye and said to me, "I wouldn't want your job." Now here I was in Denver in the night darkness. Within a few hours, I needed to say something about Columbine and God, and not just anything. It needed to be something that went straight to the heart. I did not feel up to the task. I did not feel holy enough or good enough or spiritual enough or wise enough. Yet the morning came, and we drove to the church building.

Hundreds of people were there. It seemed as though everyone was crying. I could hear the sounds all around the large room. Scripture was read, and the pastor's voice broke. Songs were sung, and we all made an effort to worship. Then I was standing at the front, feeling very small and exposed and emptied of strength and confidence. My wife prayed over me and sat down.

I suppose it was what I had been brought to Denver to do — and my family with me. Others who came in that week to speak and help undoubtedly felt the same way. I spoke from my heart and my soul and my desperation. The church taped the message, as churches often do nowadays. I have a copy of it somewhere but have never listened to it. I remember only that when the service ended, people talked with me. One young woman said, "When I showed up here this morning, I was angry. I was torn up inside. I was in pain, and I didn't know what to think or believe. Now I have hope. Thank you."

The writer of the letter to the Hebrews states, "By an act of faith, Israel walked through the Red Sea on dry ground" (Hebrews 11:29 MSG). I was no flawless saint. I won no points for a perfect attitude or a heart totally submitted to Christ. But I prayed, my wife prayed, our church back home and the church in Denver prayed. We had this little bit of faith — and this very great God.

And a road opened to us — and to others — through the storm.

FIVE

Everything was set.

Paul had planned for months. The team was prayed up and ready to go. The challenge was big—Asia.

No one had taken the gospel there before. The team only knew a few people who had been to Asia, mostly merchants, who told strange tales of strange lands with strange customs. Paul was intrigued. Was the population sparse, just a few persons scattered here and there? "Oh no," a trader told him, "Asia is teeming with people." Paul thought about this and laid it before the Lord in prayer. He felt confident enough to say to his companions, "They need to hear about Jesus. There are many people walking in darkness. Let's bring them the Light of the World."

The whole group was enthusiastic. They got what information they could from travelers and traders. Someone picked up a reliable map. They packed the essentials in their bags. One of them had memorized a smattering of phrases. *Open a road for us, Lord*, they prayed together.

So they made their way to the borderlands. But they could not cross. Nothing worked out. "They went to Phrygia," Luke remembers, "and then on through the region of Galatia. Their plan was to turn west into Asia province, but the Holy Spirit blocked that route" (Acts 16:6 MSG).

They prayed about it and carried on. "I'm sure we're meant to cross over into Asia," Paul encouraged the others. "It will happen in God's way and in God's timing. I think he wants us to enter through Bithynia."

"So they went to Mysia," writes Luke, "and tried to go north to Bithynia, but the Spirit of Jesus wouldn't let them go there either" (Acts 16:7 MSG).

A bit confused, Paul got the sense that they should head for a seaport. "Perhaps the Lord would have us make the journey on one of the trading vessels," he told the others. A little deflated, the team followed him through Mysia and then "down to the seaport Troas" (Acts 16:8 MSG).

Once they had reached Troas and found a place to stay, they ate and prayed together and then went to bed. Paul tossed and turned. *Lord, I was certain we were supposed to take your Good News into Asia. Wasn't that what you wanted us to do? Why do you keep preventing us from crossing the border? Do you want us to sail there? Where do you want us to go?*

Paul eventually fell into a restless sleep. He had a vivid dream.

A Macedonian stood on the far shore and called across the sea, "Come over to Macedonia and help us!" The dream gave Paul his map. We went to work at once getting things ready to cross over to Macedonia. All the pieces had come together. We knew now for sure that God had called us to preach the good news to the Europeans.

Acts 16:9 – 10 MSG

And to Europe the gospel went, by sailing ship from Troas. Eventually the team reached Philippi, an important city in Macedonia, and on the Sabbath they went just outside the gate to the river and a place of prayer. They spoke with several women who were meeting there. Lydia, a businesswoman, believed the gospel the team shared. She and her whole household were baptized — the first of millions who would come to follow Christ in the continent of Europe (Acts 16:11 – 15).

Paul had a plan; God had a plan. Paul wanted to reach further and further into the world with the good news about Jesus. That was the challenge, and he thought that Asia was the embodiment of that challenge. His heart was right, but he was in the wrong place. God worked at things until Paul ended up where he needed to be, then he parted the waters with a dream. Remember Israel? God worked at things until they were camped exactly where he wanted them — the Red Sea in front, the Egyptians at their back, and the desert all around. Then he split the waters, and they crossed through on dry land.

Sometimes we figure out right away where God wants us to be so he can open up a way for us we cannot open for ourselves. Other times, we get the general idea of what God is after in our lives, but we don't know the time or place we need to be so that we can watch him divide our Red Seas. The encouraging thing about Bible stories is that most of them make it clear that God is always at work behind the scenes (even in the book of Esther, in which God is never mentioned at all). Which means that if, like Paul, we are trying to do God's will and take on a big challenge we believe he's set before us, and we get mixed up about precisely what it is we're supposed to be doing, we shouldn't worry. Eventually he'll get us to where we need to be.

Is it this job, Lord? This ministry opportunity? This church? Is it this man I'm supposed to marry? This child I'm supposed to adopt? We all know the frustration of trying to figure out hard decisions and handle the big challenges when we aren't quite sure what God wants or even what is best for us. We keep running into stone walls. Dead ends. We aren't short-listed for the job we were sure God had set aside for us. The man we decide we want to marry gets engaged to someone else. The church we were certain we were called to calls somebody else. *What's going on? What are you doing, God? What am I supposed to pray about now?* The waters won't part for us.

Paul must have felt something like this during those days and weeks, maybe even months, as he dragged his team up and down the frontier, looking for God's way into Asia. The thing is, there was no such thing as God's way for him into Asia. Only Europe. But he didn't know that. For whatever reason, God often takes us the long way around, just as he did with Israel, just as he did with Paul, until whatever needs to be right in our circumstances and in us has clicked into place. There hardly ever seems to be an A to B with God without going through half the alphabet first (the A to E to Z and finally to B way of doing things). When things are right in God's eyes, often long after we thought they were right in ours, he sends the dream, or the east wind to push the waters back, or Jesus to raise the dead. The challenge has been met and overcome, but in God's way and in God's power. We think we can do it for ourselves. Then we find we can't. Then we find God's way. But it takes time.

We need to encourage ourselves and one another by remembering there's no downtime with God. There's no time that he's not working at something in our lives, that he's always got his eye out for our growth and well-being, that he's always busy getting us where we need to be, inside and out.

SIX

Suddenly the river was boiling with water and tree trunks. Soon it would roar over its banks and devour the houses that sat nearby. People were sandbagging. Soldiers were sandbagging, but no one knew if the dike would hold when the flood crested.

Our friends Sol and Crystal had a choice — stay and sandbag, trying to save their home, or make a run for it.

They had moved into the area to start a church. It met in their home, the very home the floodwaters were now threatening. It seemed wrong to just get in their car and leave. They knew God could save their home — but would he? They were familiar with Hebrews 11, the chapter of faith, and they knew the same faith that rescued some made martyrs out of others: "They were put to death by stoning; they were sawed in two; they were killed by the sword" (Hebrews 11:37 TNIV). So they had no quarrel with those who fled the neighborhood. God might stop the flood, and he might not. It simply felt wrong for them to abandon the house they'd prayed through and asked God to bless — the place in which people had met for prayer and gathered to listen to the good news about Jesus. So they stayed put and asked God to protect them, having no idea if it meant they'd wind up perched on their rooftop until a rescue team reached them.

They put their furniture up on bricks, sandbagged, fed their helpers—fellow Christians, military cadets, and strangers—and went about their chores as best they could. They talked about what was most important to save. The TV and radio were both on—the forecast was for more rain to add to the snowpack that was melting fast and tearing down out of the mountains. At night they heard the river raging and the heavy machinery growling as Cats and front-end loaders worked to shore up the berm and hold back the flood.

What was the challenge facing Sol and Crystal? That God would part the waters? They felt the challenge was more like the one that had faced Esther. She knew what the right thing to do was, and if she perished, she perished. Not that this was anything near as big a deal as what Esther was trying to do (stave off a genocide). But the idea was the same, just as it had been for Shadrach, Meshach, and Abednego. No matter what happened, Sol and Crystal wanted to trust God with the outcome. If the flood was stopped or the house ruined or many possessions lost, they wanted to be able to worship Christ as Lord in the midst of whatever occurred and believe he would bring great good out of their experience—even if disaster hit. To keep on believing through thick and thin was their Red Sea. And they wanted to pass through the waters on dry ground as believers in and worshipers of the living God.

At one point in the middle of the crisis, Sol took out his mother's Bible, a KJV encased in black Moroccan leather, opened it to Isaiah 43, and placed it on the dresser in their bedroom. They saw it dozens of times every day as they went back and forth. And every time they glanced down, they saw the words printed there:

> But now thus saith the LORD that created thee, O Jacob, and he that formed thee, O Israel, Fear not: for I have redeemed thee, I have called thee by thy name; thou art mine.
>
> When thou passest through the waters, I will be with thee; and through the rivers, they shall not overflow thee: when thou walkest through the fire, thou shalt not be burned; neither shall the flame kindle upon thee.
>
> For I am the LORD thy God, the Holy One of Israel, thy Saviour.
>
> Isaiah 43:1–3 KJV

If you ask Sol about it now, he'll shrug and smile and tell you it seemed like the right thing to do. If you push him, he'll say he felt compelled to do it. The idea came into his head, and he acted on it, opening the Bible to that passage and leaving it open until the ordeal was all over.

"It was an act of faith, I guess," he says. "We had the Bible open to those verses for all the world to see — the seen world and the unseen. We prayed that passage and we asked God to spare our home and our neighbors' homes and we asked him to continue to build his church in our house — it was holy ground. We asked that the work of the gospel not be delayed or diminished because of the flood. I don't know. Opening that Bible and leaving it open was like us saying, *We believe this promise of God and we're going to make our stand here based on that promise regardless of what goes on around us.* It was an act of faith in God, yes. But it was also an act of defiance toward our fears and the forces that played on those fears."

A bad flood had ravaged the area several years before, so everyone was expecting the worst—or almost everyone. What happened was something else: the rain turned to snow, which slowed down the rushing waters; the cooler temperatures held back the melting of the snowpack; the river, broadened by the force of the last flood, could handle a greater amount of water before spilling its banks; the storm left the area; the river shrank back from a white stone Sol had been eyeing at the top of the riverbank; and the sun emerged from behind the great hills of clouds.

Based on satellite images and the high rainfall totals, a flood should have taken place (even given the larger riverbed), because this storm had been worse than the one that had brought about the flood years before. But there was no flood. God *did* part the waters. And Sol and Crystal still have prayer meetings and Bible studies at the same house, the same holy ground, and his mother's Bible rests with other Bibles on a bookshelf, a marker placed at Isaiah 43.

SEVEN

On the surface the Red Sea looked flat and ordinary. Like any other body of water anywhere. Behind us were sand dunes and palm trees and the resort Sharm El Sheikh; in front, the Red Sea like a sheet of metal. The only thing that made me look twice were the large signs that warned of sharks, but the Swiss divers who had rented us the skin-diving equipment assured us the warnings were misleading: "There are no sharks here. We dive all the time. They are further south at Ras Mohammed. You're safe." None of us felt safe. But we slowly coaxed each other into the water just the same.

I adjusted my mask and snorkel and went under. I gasped into my mouthpiece. The bullet profile of a shark didn't cause my surprise; the beauty did.

Fish of gold and green and scarlet, fish of electric blue—schools and schools of them, like floating and flashing emeralds and sapphires and rubies. I dived, and they parted gently at my approach and then closed softly behind me, shimmering in shafts of light that had managed to pierce the sea's surface. I swam over coral reefs like rainbows and through curtains of purple and jade and indigo waters. *My God, my God, such wonders hidden under such an uninspiring sea!*

It's not that the Red Sea doesn't look lovely tucked there among the sands of Egypt, Israel, and Saudi Arabia. It's just that the sky was hazy that first day so that the sea's surface did not sparkle blue; and, considering the dramatic events that were part of its history, the shoreline did not look particularly dramatic either — no big rocks where I stood when I emerged from the water, no waves crashing into them and hurling spray at the sun, no roar, no wind, no whitecaps surging far from land.

I suppose it looked intimidating enough to the people of Israel, caught as they were between the devil and the deep blue sea, between Egyptian soldiers and a long stretch of impassable water. Yet in meeting the challenge they no longer saw the Red Sea as an obstacle, but as a passage to safety and as a guardian of their freedom: "The surging waters stood firm like a wall," they sang, "the deep waters congealed in the heart of the sea" (Exodus 15:8). And "The LORD is a warrior; the LORD is his name. Pharaoh's chariots and his army he has hurled into the sea" (Exodus 15:3–4). A challenge met in faith increases that faith, and the memory of the moment is cherished forever. It can inspire us when we face the next challenge.

On the surface, like the Red Sea that day for me, the waters of challenge can look dull, unpleasant, unpromising — and often enough grim and fearsome. Once a challenge is taken on in faith, once it is engaged or entered into, it's a different story. The strength the challenge brings to us then, the vision of God and the glory of God, the sense of God's presence, of his love and concern for us — it changes our lives.

In the same way that the Red Sea, when I dove into it, brought new visions and realities and miracles to my eyes, the Red Seas of our lifetime open us up to a new awareness of God's compassion and power and to new possibilities for our journey with our Savior through earth and eternity.

PART TWO

THE RIVERS
OF BABYLON
The WATERS of DARKNESS

By the rivers of Babylon we sat and wept
when we remembered Zion.
Psalm 137:1

ONE

The photograph is pleasant enough. As I hold it in my hand, I see the massive waterfall crashing silver into the river below. The river moves brown and green between lush banks of palm and bamboo. And it is broad, huge, so that people on the opposite shore appear much farther away than they really are. The sky is blue, with a hint of pink and gold in the west as the bright sun falls.

"Paradise," say people who look at the picture.

But I know better.

The day it was taken, a group of us had left Santa Fe de Bogotá to visit an orphanage in the jungle. I was with a group from my church, and we were in Colombia for two weeks to assist a missionary family who worked with street children, of which Bogotá had tens of thousands—boys and girls who lived, survived, and often died in the concrete jungle of the big city. The orphanage was in the real jungle, which was far less dangerous, and it fed, clothed, and schooled those children who were fortunate enough to get off the streets and into its safe and friendly environment. Part of the reason for our group's visit was to arrange sponsorship for as many of the street children as possible so the orphanage could afford to take good care of them and also be able to bring in other girls and boys.

We walked the children into town and bought them ice cream, a rare treat. They stood and sang for us in their clean school uniforms, smiles making their faces shine. Under their bright uniforms and smiles were wounds of the heart and of the body. Often off-duty police and soldiers were hired to round up street children and shoot them.

After the singing, I roamed around the orphanage and peeked into rooms and cupboards. I opened the fridges in the kitchen. It was clear the orphanage needed help, especially financial resources, for there was very little food, and what there was seemed to be of poor quality—lettuce was going black in the crispers, meat was beginning to smell, and there wasn't much of either.

I looked out from the kitchen to the children laughing and playing with our church group. I began to cry but tried hard to hide it.

It was on our way back to Bogotá, with all of this weighing on my soul, that we stopped to see the magnificent waterfall. The photographs we took that day were all true to what our eyes saw. But the photographs could not convey the smell or the history of that place.

The stench was overwhelming—of pollution, raw sewage, and rot.

What our missionary host told us of recent history at that river was overwhelming as well. Murder, slaughter, bloodshed, bodies dumped by the hundreds into the brown and green tropical waters—women, children, men, infants. Bullet holes, machete cuts, knife slashes, broken bones and necks, and purple bruises from savage beatings. So many bodies the water was stained pink, so many bodies they jammed and stalled the hydroelectric plant connected to the waterfall.

"There are probably still bodies out there," our host said with a shrug. "Down in the river mud or stuck along the bank. Rotting. Part of the stink you're breathing in."

So beautiful a river in the photograph.

So beautiful a lie.

I looked at the sweep of the river and thought of all the death and carnage it had picked up in its strong current and carried along under blue skies. I wondered how many of the bodies had been those of street children, scarcely given a chance to live, given no choice when it came time to die. I thought of the few survivors at the orphanage and of the fridges that offered only bad meat and rotting vegetables. And I said, *I am a stranger in a strange and terrible land.*

TWO

The northern kingdom of Israel had fallen to invaders from Assyria well over a hundred years before. Now it was Judah's turn to be laid waste by the armies of Babylon. "My eyes fail from weeping," agonizes Jeremiah. "I am in torment within, my heart is poured out on the ground because my people are destroyed" (Lamentations 2:11).

No one was spared. If you had been a resident of Jerusalem when it fell — and you hadn't been raped or tortured and put to the sword — you would have been taken far away into captivity, a captivity that would last for the rest of your life. You would never see your homeland again, never return to your neighborhood or attend the feast days and family celebrations you had known. You might never see your mother or father or sister or brother from the moment you were herded by soldiers into a tangled mob that was marched north. For you, life had become a life in exile while you lived on earth. You had lost the Promised Land.

"By the rivers of Babylon," the people of Israel groaned, "we sat and wept when we remembered Zion" (Psalm 137:1).

"Play us a song, one of your happy dancing songs," mocked the Babylonians. "Come on, strike up a tune. Aren't you God's chosen people? Let's see you smile and celebrate your faith!"

"Oh, how," the exiles cried, "could we ever sing GOD's song in this wasteland?" (Psalm 137:4 MSG).

And then, in a surge of anger, careful to see that their captors were not within earshot: "And you, Babylonians — ravagers! A reward to whoever gets back at you for all you've done to us; Yes, a reward to the one who grabs your babies and smashes their heads on the rocks!" (Psalm 137:8–9 MSG).

Judah had known it could happen. They just hadn't believed it. Ever since the kingdom had been divided after Solomon's death they had felt morally superior to their brothers and sisters in the north — after all, didn't they have Jerusalem as their capital? But God had sent messengers to warn them to abstain from idolatry and false gods, to separate themselves from the sexual perversions of other nations, to be just in their dealings with the poor, to make sure their courts and judges were fair and honest. Yet nothing much had changed. "We're God's people. What can happen to us?" But in time they drew down on themselves the judgment they had year after year built up against themselves. And the Babylonians came.

We can still see this sort of attitude today, not only among nations, but among Christians. If you've ever listened in on a clash between those who believe in the rapture of believers and those who don't, you may eventually hear such things as:

- "I'll wave good-bye to you as God lifts me off the earth. You'll be stuck to deal with the Antichrist on your own!"
- "I'm going to heaven to be with Jesus. I don't know where you're going!"
- "You're wrong! There *will* be a rapture. God would never let his church suffer!"

The problem with this kind of talk, quite apart from who's

right and who's wrong, is not only the spiteful attitude in which these disagreements are usually conducted but also the statements voiced as God's truth: *God would never let his church suffer!* I remember the time I heard this shouted in anger. The first image that came into my head was Christians being torn apart by lions at the Roman Coliseum.

If the story of Israel teaches us anything about suffering, it is that God's people can indeed be afflicted. In the case of the first destruction of Jerusalem (the Romans would do it again less than forty years after Christ's death and resurrection), it was something God's people brought down on their own heads. In the case of the early Christians, the persecution by Rome came as a result of faithfulness to Jesus. Two very different reasons, yet the suffering in both cases was lethal and acute.

Most of the street children of Colombia—indeed, of any country in the world—are not on the street (and sometimes stealing to survive) because they wanted it to be that way. Their parents were killed in the drug wars or by the drugs themselves or by gang leaders, military leaders, or government leaders. Or they simply abandoned their children. Or their children had to flee for their lives. It would be a hard heart that believed street children were homeless and frequently murdered because of their sins and bad choices. Most of them are victims of others' sins and bad choices.

No doubt all sorts of people went into exile when the Babylonians razed Jerusalem. Some, perhaps most, had been involved in the sorts of practices that brought about the collapse of the southern kingdom. You could say they brought the suffering on themselves. But there were probably others who hadn't done anything to defile their nation or their neighborhoods. Yet they were carried into exile as well. The many brought suffering down on all.

Not all of the German people supported the Third Reich or were Nazi Party members. A number of them actively resisted Adolf Hitler's policies and paid for it with their lives. Those who survived faced the same fate — the invasion and destruction of their country — as the Germans who had been Hitler's greatest supporters. War, famine, death, and degradation came to their doorsteps. All suffered together. No wonder many people, not just Christians, are concerned about their nations' morality and integrity. When a nation sows the wind and reaps the whirlwind, few are exempt from the national calamity that inevitably results. And this calamity can be economic, political, judicial, or anything you care to imagine, not just war and invasion.

We know this truth from our own experience. A father or mother can be careless financially, and the entire family suffers because of it. An employee feels wronged by the company he works for and shows up with a gun and shoots whomever he sees — everyone suffers because of a bad relationship between him and his boss. Friends let a friend drive under the influence — half of them wind up dead, and they take with them a family in the van they hit. A woman flicks a cigarette into the dry grass of her backyard, and the whole neighborhood goes up in flames — men, women, and children are killed. Some bring the suffering on their own heads, but some bring it down on others' heads as well.

The Christian is not exempt from making mistakes or poor choices. We can stay up late, get a cold, and suffer for it. We speed, get caught, and pay a hefty fine. Overeat for too many years, and contract heart disease. Drive too far on an empty tank, and wind up stuck out in the middle of nowhere.

Worse, a believer commits adultery and destroys his life and the life of his family. Or indulges in gossip, ruins another's life, gets confronted, and finds her own life and reputation ruined as well. A Christian steals, is caught, and then jailed, and because of a few weak moments unravels an entire lifetime of honesty and integrity. Another Christian lies habitually, and one day finds herself virtually friendless. She and others who sin become like exiles. But so do all who suffer. When we are in the middle of intense suffering, self-inflicted or not, we all feel like strangers in a strange land.

Some Christians think that no matter what problem they get into, God will fix it for them, so there's really nothing to worry about. God is a forgiving God. But knowing this truth does not erase all the consequences of mistakes and wrong behavior. I stress myself out, and I get sick—a consequence of being human. God loves me, but I remain sick. I take my paycheck and gamble it away, hoping to bring home twice as much money. I tell my wife, and we have a huge fight and she talks about divorce. God loves me, but my marriage is still in trouble. And the suffering doesn't just go away.

I once had a good friend whom I hurt, ignoring him for several months while I worked on a book. I wasn't rude or obnoxious; I just disappeared from his life without much of an explanation. When I finally emerged from my period of isolation and tried to get in touch, he would not return my calls; in fact, he wouldn't talk to me at all. This went on for months and years. It's still going on. I wrote him letters and apologized. I sent messages through mutual friends. My publisher invited him to my book launches. It didn't matter. He refused to forgive. We both suffer, and we are exiles from each other.

As a husband I can cause suffering for my wife. As a father I can cause suffering for my children. As a pastor I can cause suffering for people in the church I serve. I may not want to, but I make mistakes. Or I may do something deliberately that I know will hurt and for which I feel remorse much later. Either way, I bring suffering into the lives of those I love, and for a time we become strangers to one another.

Apologies, of course, go a long way toward making things right again. So do changes in behavior and attitude. So does knowing God forgives us in Christ and can make all things new—although the "making all things new" part usually does not happen overnight or without some effort on our part. Israel was in Babylon for many years. In time, God brought them back to their homeland. But a lot of water had to go under the bridge first, and a lot of attitudes had to change. It's often the same way with us.

Once, as a young pastor I made ill-advised remarks about a senior minister, who was also a personal friend. Why I made the remarks, I can't tell you. I know I was with a person at the time who didn't like the minister, and I got pulled into the gripe session. The thing is, I didn't even mean what I said. I liked the older pastor. But these things, as I'm sure many of you know only too well, happen. And my words came back to bite me.

The senior minister got wind of what I had said. He called me up, hurt and angry, to demand an explanation. I didn't try to dodge the bullet. I apologized for what I had said, told him I could not explain why I had been so foolish and mean-spirited, and reaffirmed my respect and affection for him. We talked for some time and were reconciled and remain fast friends to this day. Perhaps we even became stronger friends because of it, probably because he saw my genuine remorse and also heard me express my love for him in the sort of terms I wouldn't normally use except in a crisis.

The rivers of Babylon, where we find ourselves estranged from God and others and even sometimes from ourselves, provoke a suffering that is, in a way, a bit easier to comprehend and come to grips with, though the pain is no less fierce. We see it is our own actions or the actions of those close to us that have created the problem. Therefore we usually know what steps we can take to begin to rectify the situation and diminish the anguish.

It is a different matter when the rivers of God and life bring us into experiences where it is the result of our faith, and our faith alone, that horror and agony enters our home, our family, and our souls. This suffering or persecution is not easy to resolve or bring to an end; to do so we would have to give up our commitment to Christ.

THREE

It was my first home away from home after moving out of the house my parents had raised me in, an apartment close to a park at the heart of the city, and I was as proud of it as if it had been a three-story home made of glass and exotic wood and perched on a beach on the island of Maui. I wanted it to be a home in which friends and families and new faces felt welcome and could sit and talk and relax and enjoy one another and God. Yes, God was a big part of it. I prayed the one-bedroom would be a sanctuary, a holy place, a safe place, a place of worship and thankfulness. And for many months, it seemed to me, it was just that.

That summer, I left for mission work with children far north of the city. I gave a trusted friend a key to the apartment, with the suggestion he should open it up for people who needed a place to sleep or talk or pray. I never gave it another thought, for soon I was caught up in a summer of young faces, hikes, Bible stories, games, sports, and all sorts of action and adventure. Much to my surprise, a letter arrived from my friend with this statement: "I don't approve of the activities of the people you have opened your apartment up to."

This was a time before emails and cell phones, so I had to make my way to an old-time telephone and find out what was going on. After a bit of work, I managed to piece together what had happened. Since part of my ministry in the city involved working with prisoners out on parole, I had made a number of friends (and met some people who had never become friends) who had decided to take advantage of my open-door policy and take over my apartment, plucking the key from my gentle friend's hand and telling him I was OK with it. There was a lot going on in my home—drinking and drugs, for example—that I'd always told visitors wasn't part of the deal if they wanted to hang out at my place. Not being able to get an answer when I called my apartment, I spoke to a friend who worked alongside me in the prison ministry and asked him to tell them to move out until I could come and assess the situation. He promised to do as I asked.

But it was too late. The prisoners hadn't only been drinking and smoking up and popping pills; they'd been planning an armed robbery at a large bank. My home had become a place for guns, bullets, sniper scopes, and schemes. Only days before the hit on the bank was to take place, a SWAT team raided my apartment—the police had been keeping an eye on the parolees all along. Everyone was arrested and hustled back behind concrete walls and iron bars. I came back from my mission in the north to an apartment turned upside down, thoroughly ransacked by the police and strewn with other people's clothing, dirty dishes, cigarette and marijuana butts, pornography, and empty boxes of high-powered rifle cartridges. The holy had become unholy. I had scarcely walked in the door and taken a long look before I knelt in the rubbish of my home and wept before God.

If I hadn't been involved in ministry to prisoners, this wouldn't have happened. If I hadn't tried to bring the gospel to inmates on parole, this wouldn't have happened. If I hadn't opened my door to people who desperately needed Jesus, this wouldn't have happened. As I sorted out feelings of pain, anger, betrayal, and anguish, both on my knees and on my feet, I realized I might as well have added, *Jesus came to earth, and he too faced the darkness of dealing with people caught in sin's grip. Yet if Jesus hadn't come to earth and faced that darkness and died on the cross, he never would have saved a single soul.*

Love for the world had brought Jesus into harm's way. Love for Jesus and the things Jesus loved had brought me into harm's way. It brings all Christians into harm's way at one time or another. Is there really any way of getting around that and still being a follower of Christ? Reading the New Testament, it didn't look like it to me. So, still hurt and angry, I went back on my knees to pray for people, some who had been friends and some not, who for a time had acted like enemies toward me.

God was not asking me to agree with what they had done. He was not asking me to take it lightly. He was not even asking me not to be upset. He was simply asking me to pray for them and to forgive them and to not give up on them. So I tried to do that. It did not come easy, and it did not happen overnight, but bit by bit, I got there, for I came to see that God had forgiven me as well and had never given up on the person he hoped I would become in Christ.

I never understood why the police didn't arrest me as well — after all, the apartment was in my name — or at least bring me in for questioning. I found out later that several of the inmates had wanted to pull me down with them, but others flat-out told the police, "Look, this guy had nothing to do with it. He had no idea what was going on. We knew he was away, so we got the key to his place and planned the whole robbery behind his back. Leave the man alone." And the police did. For several weeks, I saw a patrol car parked out in the street under my window, but no officer ever approached me or came to my door. And then one day, the patrol car was gone.

I received letters from some of the prisoners, and at least one put me on his visitors' list, but that fall I left for college and never saw any of them again. In one sense, I dropped the ball, because even though I forgave them, I still did not have the strength or grace to pass through those prison gates and face them. In another sense, it was all over, and I had moved on to a different place and different challenges. I gave up the apartment — the place I'd been so proud of and enjoyed so much for such a short time. Before I left, I walked to the river that flowed not far from the apartment complex. I looked at the water and wondered about all the pain and loss and whether any good fruit had come out of what had taken place.

I'd learned more about forgiveness and praying for those who betrayed me. I discovered that when you prayed for your enemies, in Christ's "water into wine" way, they became your companions. Maybe the prisoners had also learned some things about God and his love for them, I didn't know. People had asked me if I would ever work with street people again, with the poor, with prisoners. They wondered if I even wanted to be involved in Christian ministry again. As I stood by my own river of Babylon and watched ice forming at its sides, I realized the answer was a foregone conclusion.

You either believed in Jesus as Savior and Lord or you didn't. If you did, you followed him, and that could take you anywhere and to anyone at any time. Who knew what sort of places you'd end up living in or the kind of people Jesus would ask you to love and care for in his name? If you didn't want to accept that risk, you didn't pick up your cross and follow him. It was as simple as that. Despite the suffering I had gone through and the inkling that I would go through even more suffering for Jesus, it really came down to who or what my God would be, not whether there would be more hurt and betrayal in my life because of my faith. And once it came down to whom I was going to serve, it became something of an obvious choice. Peter took the words out of my mouth when he responded to Jesus' question about leaving him: "Lord, to whom shall we go? You have the words of eternal life. We have come to believe and to know that you are the Holy One of God" (John 6:68–69 TNIV).

FOUR

For some, the suffering of defeat and exile was compounded when their commitment to the God of Israel brought severe persecution. The rivers of Babylon — of which the Tigris and the Euphrates are the largest — saw more than just weeping and moaning and a broken people who would not sing. They also saw great faith rising out of the suffering of captivity.

There is the story of the prophet Ezekiel. All his visions and messages took place in exile, including his famous account of the Spirit of God in Ezekiel 1:

> I looked: I saw an immense dust storm come from the north, an immense cloud with lightning flashing from it, a huge ball of fire glowing like bronze. Within the fire were what looked like four creatures vibrant with life. Each had the form of a human being, but each also had four faces and four wings.
>
> Ezekiel 1:4–6 MSG

Ezra, Nehemiah, and Esther are stories of faith in captivity, although by this time the Babylonians have been defeated and the Persian Empire rules the Babylonian lands and its peoples.

Daniel also gives us several accounts of faith emerging from the exile and experiences of persecution. The most famous are the stories of Shadrach, Meshach, and Abednego and of Daniel in the lions' den.

Shadrach and his companions are in the service of the king of Babylon, Nebuchadnezzar. The king has an image of gold cast, ninety feet high by nine feet wide. He orders everyone to bow down and worship it when music is played. But Shadrach and the others will not compromise their faith in God. This gets them in trouble. Enraged, the king snarls, "If you do not worship it, you will be thrown immediately into a blazing furnace. Then what god will be able to rescue you from my hand?" (Daniel 3:15).

It's almost as if the three men answer with a shrug:

> "Your threat means nothing to us. If you throw us in the fire, the God we serve can rescue us from your roaring furnace and anything else you might cook up, O king. But even if he doesn't, it wouldn't make a bit of difference, O king. We still wouldn't serve your gods or worship the gold statue you set up."
>
> Daniel 3:16–18 MSG

The king goes wild with fury and orders the furnace stoked up seven times hotter than normal. Soldiers bind the three with rope and throw them in. They do not die. The ones who threw them in do. But they walk among the flames unharmed.

Nebuchadnezzar is stunned not only by this but by seeing a fourth man walking in the fires — one he says "looks like a son of the gods" (Daniel 3:25). He orders Shadrach and his two friends out of the furnace. They are not hurt, not so much as singed. Their clothing is not burnt; they don't even have the smell of smoke on them.

"Praise be to the God of Shadrach, Meshach and Abednego," cries Nebuchadnezzar, "who has sent his angel and rescued his servants! They trusted in him and defied the king's command and were willing to give up their lives rather than serve or worship any god except their own God" (Daniel 3:28). Then in typical Nebuchadnezzar fashion, he commands that anyone anywhere who treats the three men's God with contempt will "be cut into pieces and their houses be turned into piles of rubble" (3:29). He decides there is no god like their God because no other god can save like their God. So the persecution of the three men leads to a blessing that not only bolsters their faith—if it needed any bolstering—but also brings the king of a pagan empire to acknowledge the supremacy of the one true God.

Daniel in the lions' den is a story along the same lines, only this time the king is Persian, and he is tricked into putting Daniel in harm's way. King Darius is encouraged to issue a thirty-day decree that no one can pray to anyone or anything except him. It is a trap to get Daniel, who serves the king and his government, but the king doesn't realize this until he is confronted with the news that Daniel is still praying to his God three times a day. He tries to save Daniel, but the law cannot be altered. So Daniel is flung among the hungry lions, and all Darius can say is, "May your God, whom you serve continually, rescue you!" (Daniel 6:16).

God does. Daniel lives through the night, and like Shadrach and his friends, no wound is found on him. Darius has Daniel's accusers and their families thrown into the den, where they are killed. And like Nebuchadnezzar, he decrees that everyone within his empire must treat the God of Daniel with reverence: "For he is the living God and he endures forever; his kingdom will not be destroyed, his dominion will never end" (Daniel 6:26). Once again, persecution ends with a blessing that not only saves the one persecuted but brings another king of a pagan empire to acknowledge the supremacy of the one true God. Daniel's brief period of suffering, as in the case of Shadrach, Meshach, and Abednego, brings about something far greater than the suffering endured.

Of course, the stories don't always end this way, not in Scripture, not in life. Prophets were slain in the Old Testament; Stephen was persecuted and murdered in the New; Peter and Paul and many other Christians were slaughtered by the Roman Empire. In the same breath as the writer of Hebrews 11 tells us how believers were saved by their faith, he goes on to describe how others were killed for their faith.

Many books detail story after story of Christians martyred in the former Soviet Union, in Communist China, in North Korea, in Islamic republics. Missionaries were abducted and killed in Colombia only a short time before I arrived with the team from our church. In the summer of 2008, a young Saudi woman was condemned to death for converting to Christianity — her tongue was cut out, and she was burned alive by her own father. That fall, in Nigeria, Muslim extremists killed six pastors and destroyed forty church buildings. At the same time, in the state of Orissa in India, dozens of Christians were murdered by Hindu mobs. Pick a country, pick an era—including the twenty-first century—and you will find stories about Christians who suffer for no other reason than the fact they worship the living God revealed in the person of Jesus Christ.

Most of us are not going to get shot or burned or drowned or stoned for our faith in Jesus. But we feel a hint of persecution just the same—in the way we are treated at the office or at school, the slights aimed at us at town halls or political rallies, our opinions ignored at discussions among relatives or acquaintances. Sometimes, of course, it can get more intense than that. It all depends on where you live and who you know and who knows you.

The idea behind all the stories of believers in the Bible who are suffering for their faith is that their faithfulness and commitment are bigger things than their persecution. Suffering for righteousness is a triumph. How odd this sounds to many of us, for we would do almost anything to avoid pain and harassment on account of our Christian faith. Yet this is exactly how the first Christians saw it: "The apostles left the Sanhedrin, rejoicing because they had been counted worthy of suffering disgrace for the Name" (Acts 5:41). Peter writes, "Rejoice that you participate in the sufferings of Christ, so that you may be overjoyed when his glory is revealed. If you are insulted because of the name of Christ, you are blessed, for the Spirit of glory and of God rests on you" (1 Peter 4:13–14). Paul longs to know Christ "and the fellowship of sharing in his sufferings" (Philippians 3:10). He says that we share in Christ's sufferings "in order that we may also share in his glory" (Romans 8:17). In his letter to the Christians at Philippi, he makes it clear and simple: "It has been granted to you on behalf of Christ not only to believe on him, but also to suffer for him" (Philippians 1:29).

Suffering as a Christian for being a Christian apparently goes hand in hand with embracing Jesus as Savior and Lord. It is not pleasant but neither would it be as frightening or mystifying to us when persecution rears its head if we were familiar with the biblical teaching concerning its inevitability—and its reward. Just as the cross is the heart of our salvation so too carrying the cross for Christ seems to be at the heart of our faith: "Whoever wants to be my disciple," says Jesus, "must deny themselves and take up their cross daily and follow me. For whoever wants to save their life will lose it, but whoever loses their life for me will save it. What good is it for you to gain the whole world, and yet lose or forfeit your very self?" (Luke 9:23–25 TNIV). If we don't carry the cross, we are not worthy of Christ, and we cannot call ourselves Christians (Matthew 10:38; Luke 14:27).

We don't go looking for persecution or asking for our faith to be tested by fire. We simply live the Christian life, and the persecution and fire will find us soon enough. What we need to do is encourage one another that none of us should find it odd when we suffer for our faith. Expecting that our commitment to Jesus will usher in a complete absence of persecution is a wrong way of looking at the Christian journey and the opposite of what Scripture teaches. "Do not be surprised at the fiery ordeal that has come on you to test you," Peter tells us, "as though something strange were happening to you" (1 Peter 4:12 TNIV). It's part and parcel of the Christian experience—not simply suffering that results from accidents and disease because we're human, or because we make mistakes and bad life choices or commit sins. Suffering for our faith in Jesus is different. It's a given and also a privilege. They did the same to your Master; they will do the same to you. In this way, your persecutors do you the honor of connecting you unmistakably to Jesus Christ. "If we endure," Paul recites in 2 Timothy 2:12, "we will also reign with him." And Dietrich Bonhoeffer, a German pastor who perished under the Nazi regime, adds, remembering Paul, "Those who love the cross of Jesus Christ, those who have genuinely found peace in it, now begin to love even the tribulations in their lives, and ultimately will be able to say with Scripture, 'We also boast in our sufferings.'"*

---

* Dietrich Bonhoeffer, *Meditations on the Cross* (Louisville: Westminster, 1998), 41.

FIVE

When Jack wanted to be alone, he went to the river.

He grew up just north of the Dakotas, and two mighty rivers met in his city at a place called The Forks — the Red and the Assiniboine. It was the Assiniboine that flowed from west to east only a few blocks from his house. He would walk down to where it passed through a large park and sit on the bank and watch it move, sometimes swiftly, sometimes slowly.

The Assiniboine froze in the winter, and people shoveled off the snow and skated and played hockey on it. In the spring, during breakup, large chunks of ice swept down the river like massive sailing ships. Some took on frightening shapes; others looked as soft and white as down. He watched and thought for hours, a weak spring sun draping his head and falling across the backs of his hands.

During the worst time of his life, Jack came to the river with whatever faith he could muster to pray and listen to the Maker of the world and the Savior of his soul — his Master and Lord and the God of the waters. It was a little like what he had read in a Winnie the Pooh book as a child: "Sometimes, if you stand on the bottom rail of a bridge and lean over to watch the river slipping slowly away beneath you, you will suddenly know everything there is to be known."

It began with his younger brother's birth—a boy meant to be a companion for Jack since Jack's other brother was five years older and his sister eight years older. On that day, the black-and-white TV was on, and aunts filled his house because Mom and Dad were at the hospital preparing for Scotty's birth. A few days later, when they brought him through the door, he was wonderful—blonde hair, skin softer and smoother and gentler than anything Jack had ever touched. Jack wasn't even three years old, and he was overjoyed.

But there had been problems. The umbilical cord had been wrapped around Scotty's neck while he was in the womb; as a result he was paralyzed along one side of his body. They called his condition cerebral palsy. There should have been a C-section. There wasn't, and now Scotty would never walk, never talk, never run. But he could laugh and love and swing his body and head from side to side to show his delight—and this was more than enough for Jack. As they grew up together, they would play for hours at a time. One of Scotty's favorite games was making a tower of tins and pots and then rolling lids into it and knocking the tower down with a crashing and a jangling and a banging that thrilled him.

Other things were going on that Jack didn't know about. His mother felt guilty about Scotty's crippling condition. There were fights with Jack's father—they had hardly ever fought before. Once she threatened to stab him with a fork. He pinned her arms to her sides, knocked away the fork, forced her backward into their bedroom, and threw her on the bed. She kicked out at him. Jack was hanging on the back of his father with all of his might to try to keep him from pushing his mom. His sister and brother were trying to stop the fight too, shouting and crying. When his mother later went to sit on the couch in the living room, Jack sat at her feet. Tears welled up in her eyes; tears spilled down his face. She looked out the large picture window for hours, and he stayed there next to her.

Years later, Jack was drawing cartoons in the dining room when his mom screamed she couldn't take it anymore and tried to run out the back door. Jack's dad blocked her flight, but she broke away and crashed through the front door, falling down the steps on to the grass. As she lay there crying, neighbors came, as did an ambulance. Friends asked, "Your mom broke her leg, didn't she?" Jack nodded, fearful they might find out what had really happened. The ambulance took her away, and she didn't come back.

No one took the time to explain to Jack what had just gone on and where his mother was going and when she'd be coming back. He was left alone in his room — this vulnerable nine-year-old boy. Suddenly his dad had to not only carry on with his full-time job but also be a single parent at a time when there weren't many single parents — and certainly not many male ones.

Frustration came to a boiling point in the father's head and heart. He fought with Jack's brother and sister. He beat Jack — using his fists or a belt buckle. Jack's clothes covered all of the wounds. No one knew. But when Jack undressed for his baths, the sight of bruises of all shapes and colors — some red and purple, some green, some yellow — assaulted his eyes. When he looked at these bruises behind a closed door, tears of anger and pain roared out of him, and with a horrible fury he punched the stacks of towels neatly folded on the shelves above the toilet, too young and weak to lash out at his father. "What has happened," he raged, "to the man who used to bake potatoes for me when we burned the autumn leaves, who rented a cottage on the lake for our family in the summer, who told me stories and hugged me against his warm, gray sweater?"

One day, the dad threw Jack's older brother down on the floor in the hall and strangled him. The sounds of choking were loud and terrifying. His brother's crime had been to get mud all over his new shoes. Another time, as they ate the lunch his dad had prepared, Scotty got in the way—Scotty was always on the floor crawling from room to room. Jack's dad kicked him again and again in a burst of anger. Scotty did not cry. But Jack did. He and his brother and sister kept their heads down in pain and shame, and his tears fell into the soup he spooned into his mouth.

Jack's mother was in an asylum for months. She received shock treatment. Different aunts came to stay with the family at various times and help out, making the home feel even stranger and colder. At some point, the government decided Scotty could not be cared for properly at home, and he was taken away and placed in an institution. With his mother and younger brother gone, it felt like the end of the world in Jack's heart.

Jack used to wander up and down the back lanes and alleys just to get away—yes, and to sit by the river. His mother finally returned home, but then she would get ill again and return to the asylum. At school, a favorite phrase to fling at someone was "you retard!" Every time Jack heard it, he thought of Scotty (who was labeled as "severely retarded") and absorbed another blow. Another joke was to say someone belonged in a nuthouse. "Hey, Jack, you belong in ..." — and they would shout the name of the place in which his mother was hospitalized. Home was hard; in a way school was harder.

His mom returned home to stay, but not Scotty. Since the family did not own a car, they had to take a combination of bus routes to go to see him. His parents went every Saturday and Sunday. Jack joined them sometimes, but it was difficult. He hated the institution and the smell of the floor cleansers. He was upset to hear his parents whisper that some of the staff slapped Scotty. So he never felt good there. But now and then he went, and it was wonderful to see Scotty again. But it was never like being at home — never.

In time, his mother became a Christian, and soon after he did too. He and his mom prayed constantly for Scotty's healing. The problem was that her church had the idea that Scotty would be healed instantly if his mother only had enough faith that it would happen. Scotty wasn't healed right away, so it must have meant that his mother didn't have enough faith. She had always felt his crippling in her womb had been her fault; now she was to blame for the fact he wasn't healed too. Even though Jack was a young Christian, he knew she had received wrong teaching, and he tried to talk his mom out of accepting it. But she believed the church, not her son. She grew depressed. A psychiatrist filled her cupboards with pills. She began to smoke and to gain weight — too much weight. And Jack went to the river and prayed.

God, one day it will be like it used to be. No, it will be better, because my brother will be healed, my mom will be healed, my dad and brother and sister will believe. It will be incredible.

It was when Jack was twenty-one and Scotty about nineteen that Jack went traveling for a year. He wound up at a kibbutz in Israel. In those days, his country's postal workers went on strike frequently for higher wages. For months, volunteers at the kibbutz from all over the world got mail daily, while Jack received nothing—until one day the mail started flowing again. He was afraid to open his letters. It had been so long he was certain he would get bad news. His mother's first letter confirmed his sense of dread. Scotty had been hit by a seizure. For him to have a seizure wasn't unusual, but this time he went into a coma and died.

Jack went out into the orchards where he harvested oranges, and under the moon that had shone on Israel for thousands of years, he wept as David had wept over Jonathan and Absalom, as Jeremiah had wept for the slain of Jerusalem, as Jesus had wept for Lazarus, as Rachel had wept for her children, refusing to be comforted "because her children are no more" (Jeremiah 31:15).

Oh, my Lord, wouldn't it have been better if Scotty had been healed—better for my mother, my father, my family, better for all who would hear the story and the testimony? Wouldn't it have brought honor to your name? My God, my God, where are you?

So Jack returned home. Life went on. Its flow never ceases for anyone or anything. In time, he met a young woman and fell in love. In time they were married; in time they moved to a part of the country far from either of their families. Jack continued to pray for his mother's healing, for she struggled with depression, excessive weight, diabetes, and smoking, and she was also having trouble getting her breath. In time, a phone call came—the kind of phone call we all know only too well—and Jack stood in a violent red dawn after a night of grief that felt like stab wounds and cried out to God once more.

God, wouldn't Mom's healing have been a great blessing? Wouldn't it have been better than her death? Wouldn't it have brought my family to faith? Wouldn't it have made this a better world than the one I am standing in right now?

Jack and his wife drove all day and all night to get to Jack's hometown. The autopsy revealed that his mother had died from an overdose of pills.

Home, yes, home to the father he loved—the father who had beaten him, the father Jack had forgiven even as God had forgiven him, the father he wanted to comfort and hold, the father he prayed for every day of his life.

And in time, cancer took the father, and the story ended.

SIX

Deep calls to deep
in the roar of your waterfalls;
all your waves and breakers
have swept over me....

Your wrath lies heavily on me;
you have overwhelmed me with all your waves....

Your wrath has swept over me;
your terrors have destroyed me.
All day long they surround me like a flood;
they have completely engulfed me.
You have taken from me friend and neighbor—
darkness is my closest friend.

Psalms 42:7; 88:7, 16–18 TNIV

Sometimes the river overflows its banks—not because of sin or because we're being persecuted for our faith. It's like the suffering of Job—there is no good reason for it. It brings to mind the question Asaph asked:

What's going on here? Is God out to lunch?
Nobody's tending the store.
The wicked get by with everything;
they have it made, piling up riches.

I've been stupid to play by the rules;
*   what has it gotten me?*
A long run of bad luck, that's what—
*   a slap in the face every time I walk out the door.*
                    Psalm 73:11 – 14 MSG

Jack's story is a true story. All the names have been changed. But what happened, happened. And although God has brought about much healing, questions still remain and probably always will this side of heaven. Why did his family suffer so much? Why wasn't his younger brother healed? Why did the only other Christian in the family—his own mother—commit suicide?

We all have our hard stories, and we're familiar with the hard stories of others. We try to make sense of the almost insane suffering some people go through, but in the end we can't connect the dots. We just don't see the full picture. Whatever perspective God has, we don't have it. We are left with a choice to live by faith or not—faith that God is good and that in all things he works for the good of his children, whether it's obvious to us or not.

While I was at university, a pastor-friend and fellow student who worked with men at a maximum security prison was gunned down by his own nephew. The young man had a problem with drugs, and my friend was trying to help him. My friend—a young man himself—left behind a wife and children. The nephew was caught and placed in the same prison my friend had ministered in.

A dynamic and sensitive evangelist, one whom I'd met and spoken with personally and at length, was preparing to reach out in thoughtful and loving ways to the great city he lived in. I knew this would be very interesting because he was considered "the thinking man's evangelist," someone who took the time to consider the hard questions and talk about them with those who did not believe. Months before this outreach was to take place, he was found dead in his office—heart attack, brain aneurism, I can't remember which. The outreach never took place. There really was no one else like him.

A teacher at one of my alma maters, a true Christian gentleman and still young, was writing important books for the Christian community that helped believers wrestle with some of the hard issues of the early years of the twenty-first century. He was particularly special to me because he encouraged me to write and to study, even to pursue a doctorate if that was God's will. I would phone him once or twice a year to get spiritual shots in the arm. He was always gracious and encouraging. One day, without warning, he collapsed from a brain aneurism and was placed on a respirator. After a day or two, when there was no sign of life, no sign of hope, they disconnected him from the apparatus. And the books he hadn't finished remained unfinished.

A friend and his wife had been working with youth and street children in a city near me for several years. Then they went to Africa to work with the orphans of parents who had died from AIDS. He was a bundle of holy electricity, always on the move, always serving, always concocting another plan, bursting with faith and compassion. The doctors had said he and his wife would never have children, but then, miraculously, she became pregnant, and they were filled with joy, looking forward to their child's birth. During the Christmas holiday season, he woke up gasping and choking. His heart had given way; his body had broken down. His wife and friends applied CPR. But he died. And his son was born in the spring.

We often try to find reasons for our suffering. We have a need to find out what greater purpose it serves. Sometimes we glimpse a pattern, but most of the time we are at a loss to explain the things that hurt us most. We read Job and realize the only answer Job got in the end was God himself. We try to come up with a formula, but God is no formula. Job's comforters had a formula. They tried to make everything fit, and they were wrong. In the end, we run up against Deuteronomy 29:29: The things God reveals to us are ours to hold on to and live by forever, but the hidden things are his business.

This is hard to swallow for those who have been taught they should be able to figure everything out. But there is no escaping the harsh reality of this planet. We won't comprehend everything this side of eternity. We will not see the resolution of every painful episode in our lives. We will never be capable of grasping everything God can grasp unless he chooses to reveal it to us. We are left with choosing to believe in a good God — or not — regardless of the circumstances.

It is common among Christians to talk about the redemptive role of suffering, that it makes us better people, deeper people. "Suffering produces perseverance," writes Paul in Romans 5:3 – 4, "perseverance, character; and character, hope." It can. But suffering can also leave people angry, embittered, and empty of faith. One person loses a child yet becomes a wellspring of faith and hope to others; another becomes a pit of poison, an embodiment of hatred, cynicism, and unbelief. We go where our faith or lack of faith takes us. All of us know people who have chosen one path or the other. And if not for the grace of God, most of us would wind up emotional and spiritual wrecks when suffering ravages our lives.

But we thank God because there *is* his grace, and if we accept it, we find that his unconditional love is what makes the difference between heaven or hell in our lives. Jack had no idea he would ever be able to forgive his father. Had he been strong enough the day his father kicked his younger brother, he believes he would have attacked his father and killed him. Even now, when he relives those painful memories, he finds it easier to forgive the blows his father rained on him than the blows that were rained on his little brother. Nevertheless, long before his father died of cancer, Jack was able to hug and kiss his father, tell him he loved him, and mean it.

"Only Jesus could have done that in my life," Jack says, "because only Jesus suffered in a way that makes sense to me. And that makes me feel he understands my own pain."

Sometimes we overlook the phrase from Isaiah 53 that tells us the Messiah, Jesus, would be "a man of sorrows, and acquainted with grief" (Isaiah 53:3 KJV). But such a view of Jesus made an enormous difference to Jack. Jesus knew what sorrow was. And he not only knew what grief was; he was intimately acquainted with it. It cut right into his heart. He was not just a happy, dancing Savior; he was someone who knew very well what it was to be bent with sadness and to grieve deeply.

This was a person Jack could understand and, even more importantly, someone who could understand Jack and help him.

So it helped to have this "man of sorrows" alongside when Jack gripped the hard rocks of his life with both hands and tried to move them. For instance, it was much harder for him to come to terms with his brother's death and his mother's suicide than his father's beatings. Why didn't God intervene? Jack knew God could heal—indeed, his father's first bout with cancer, twenty years before his death from a different onslaught, had resulted in a clean recovery so astounding that the doctor, not a believer in such things, had said the healing was miraculous. Jack had prayed for that very thing for his father, so he knew God could deliver. Why then didn't God heal his mother and brother too?

The idea of God's selective intervention—that the Lord chooses to intervene and heal some but not all—caused Jack a great deal of trouble at first. He could see why some people felt God didn't like them if he healed suffering in another person's family but not in theirs. He came to realize that God had reasons he could not explain to Jack because Jack, in his mortal state, did not have the capacity to understand. A hard pill for proud humans to swallow, especially if they think they are gods themselves and subject to no limitations, but Jack came to embrace it as the truth. The honey that helped the pill go down was Jesus weeping at the grave of Lazarus; Jesus weeping over Jerusalem; Jesus filled with grief at the plight of the widow of Nain, who had lost her only son; Jesus cut with sorrow at the suffering and confusion of human beings, who were like terrified sheep without a shepherd. The clincher was Jesus crucified, looking down at his killers and asking the Father to forgive them—something Jack had found so hard to do in the case of his own father.

For Jack, the God he embraced in Jesus was not a distant deity but a friend close at hand, who felt hurt as much as Jack did. He came to believe that Jesus not only knew and understood his grief over his brother's final seizure and his mother's suicide but grieved also—even though he was all-powerful—just as he had grieved over Lazarus and the widow and many others while he was on earth. This belief gave Jack a comfort and peace he had not known on his journey—God was not above crying with him during the cruel seasons of life, not because God was helpless, but because there were things that could not be expressed in a way Jack would understand and because God knew how much Jack suffered with both his pain and his inability to comprehend any purpose behind that pain. The reality of Jesus suffering and dying on Calvary for others only brought home God's empathy and compassion even more completely to him.

"You could write books about this stuff," Jack told me, "but in the end the only answer to the suffering of the human race is Christ dying on the cross." Jane Kenyon, New Hampshire's poet laureate when she died of leukemia in 1995, agrees with him. In a poem she calls *Looking at Stars*, she writes:

> *The God of curved space, the dry*
> *God, is not going to help us, but the son*
> *whose blood spattered*
> *the hem of his mother's robe.**

---

* Jane Kenyon, *Collected Poems* (St. Paul, Minn.: Graywolf, 2005), 210.

SEVEN

Our infant daughter, who wasn't gaining weight and had colic, suddenly began losing what weight she had. Filled with fear, we prayed and tried everything we could think of, including everything the doctors could think of. My wife and I drove her to the children's hospital an hour away, following the bends and straight runs of a strong river that flowed east out of the mountains. At the hospital we entered a wing I had never been in before.

As our daughter underwent tests, we waited and paced. Our pacing took us past rooms with children in them, and it soon became clear that these children were dealing with serious health issues. Many had their heads shaved, and IV lines ran from heads and arms. Most were pale. Some walked; some lay in beds; some sat. There was no laughing, very little smiling—hardly any sounds at all. Parents walked with their children, who usually had a silver IV pole rattling alongside, but even that rattling took on a subdued tone.

Often I would see parents, with eyes like dark holes, sag onto a chair or couch in a large waiting area. The lighting was soft, and the space was heavily carpeted. Our shoes made little noise, and everyone spoke in a kind of hush. Nurses and others I concluded were counselors often sat next to defeated parents and tried to speak with them.

What would I as a pastoral counselor say to them? What would I say about their children being struck down so young, their lives brief and much of that time spent in suffering? What words were there? Perhaps there were no human words. Only divine ones. If we could open ourselves up enough to God, couldn't we all hear them?

Eventually, Israel returned to the Promised Land. Their suffering and exile had made the generation that returned a people different from the ones who had been conquered. There would be years of rebuilding, of prosperity and peace. Yet great suffering would come to Israel again.

And so it comes to us also. Though some bear more of a burden than others, we all receive our share in our lifetimes. How will we shoulder it? And whose shoulder will we find to help us? With what sort of heart, what sort of faith, will we try to make our way back to a life that has more promise, stability, and joy?

Jack would tell us we needed a relationship with Jesus far deeper than any relationship we'd had with anyone before. He'd tell us to look forward to a day when our loved ones would stand before us, smiling, more real than the world we live in now. He'd tell us it all hung on Jesus Christ — what he said and did for us, and all the things he still says and does for us. "In this world you will have trouble," Jack would quote from John 16:33, reminding us of words Jesus shared only hours before his own suffering and death, "but take heart! I have overcome the world."

PART THREE

RIVERS IN
THE DESERT

The WATERS *of* REJUVENATION

Restore our fortunes, O LORD,
like streams in the Negev.
Psalm 126:4

ONE

She told me how the thunder season came to Arizona — lightning igniting the skies, explosions rocking the mountains, and rain coming hard and fast like silver-tipped spears. Barren sand would soak up the water. An area that was nothing more than empty wasteland the day before would suddenly burst into color, like flames erupting across a dry field.

"For years we were never there when the rains came," she explained, "so I'd never seen any of these flowers before. Then when Hank died, I went there on my own, and I stayed longer than normal. You talk about the wilderness blooming like a rose, well, that's what happens in Arizona when the rains come."

I told her that the rains came to Israel in the winter. The riverbeds or wadis that I loved to hike through during the summer months became dangerous once the skies opened. A wadi that was dry and empty in the morning could be a raging torrent by the afternoon, sweeping away everything in its path.

She nodded. "They call them arroyos, and the same thing happens. It's pouring in the mountains, and after a few hours all that water has to find an outlet, and it fills up the arroyos and turns them into rivers. People get killed. They're hiking in there, you know, sometimes even camping, and they think they're safe because it's not raining where they are, but they forget about what's happening up in the mountains. Oh, there are signs posted all over the place warning you in English and in Spanish, but people ignore them. Even the locals get caught sometimes."

"But the water brings life to others."

"Yes, it does, doesn't it? The animals, the birds, trees and shrubs, and people."

I spoke about how beautiful the walls of the wadis were in the Middle East; how the water, with all its force, chiseled and carved and smoothed and created incredible lines and patterns, brought out colors in the stone that no one knew were there.

She smiled and thought out loud about what she had seen in the arroyos — sculptings and shapings, art that fascinated and startled the eye, light that dazzled and made you feel you'd been pulled into the heart of the sun, shafts and beams of brilliance that stood at curves in the riverbeds like guardian angels, shadows that touched the skin of one's face like a cool cloth and made paintings on the stone.

"There is danger when the rains come," she told me, "but most of all, the rivers of the desert bring life — and it's always a sudden rush and always a great surprise."

TWO

I was told the church was simply an aging congregation that needed some encouragement and an influx of younger families. So after a few discussions with the church board, my wife and I moved to the area. The region was lapped by salt water and ribboned with creeks and swift rivers fed by mountains and a large inland glacier. It was lush and green and ripe with beauty. The word *paradise* came to mind. The two of us felt at home immediately.

I heard some rumors about its reputation as a cult church, but I had no idea what this gossip was based on. I became the pastor and friend of many older people. Many sermons were preached, many homes visited, many Bible studies and prayer meetings led, and many potlucks eaten. Our early days began much the same as any new church pastorate begins.

There was one thing. The majority of the people in the church belonged to an organization that, as far as I knew, was just another group that raised money for various charities. It was only after a few months that I began to hear some whispers that my sermons were flawed because I taught that Jesus was Savior and Lord, that he was the way and the truth and the life. I made a man out to be God incarnate, and I made that same man out to be the Savior of the world. This, of course, is standard belief for not only an evangelical church but any church that takes the Bible and Jesus Christ seriously. There was no great uprising so I shrugged my shoulders, prayed to Christ for wisdom and strength, and carried on.

Now it seems that former pastors of churches don't always disappear. In this case, the former pastor was also the founding pastor, and he wanted to retire in the lovely valley in which the church was situated—and keep coming to the church. I was OK with that, until I found out he chaired a meeting in my absence one evening and fielded complaints about my focus on Jesus Christ. I talked with my leadership team pretty strongly about this painful incident but, in an effort to make peace, agreed to participate in the founding pastor's special Good Friday service he was planning for his charitable organization.

It was a stormy day when I pulled into the church parking lot. The lot was full of cars, and a large number of men milled about wearing strange white robes and headgear. Inside, there were oaths made with fists clenched over the heart, the words recited almost like a shout. The order of service was like nothing I'd ever seen before. Little was made of Jesus' sacrifice on the cross. Somewhere in there I was asked to do a prayer. I drove home depressed and perplexed.

So I began to read up on the organization. I was astonished to discover that even at the lowest level, blood oaths were required with sweeping motions of the hands: I will cut out my heart and lungs and slash my throat if I ever reveal the secrets of this brotherhood. I found out that Jesus was considered a good man, a teacher and prophet on a par with Moses and Buddha and Mohammed, but no more than that. The thing that mattered, that must be preserved, was the global brotherhood that embraced all religions as similar paths to God. I found oaths for higher levels—there were many levels one could aspire to in this organization—that created new names for God, new names that often involved mixing in old names, like the titles for pagan gods and goddesses cited in the Old Testament as abominations that Israel must avoid. It was a bewildering education for me, but it did shed light on what I was dealing with at this church.

I had been struggling with insomnia and feelings of oppression and claustrophobia for months and had attributed this to the weather—the area had a rainy, cloudy winter. Now I wondered if there might be more to it. My wife and I read the Word and prayed and sometimes fasted. Then came the envelope containing the invitation to join the organization.

It would make life easier in one sense. I'd be one of them, and perhaps the sense of impending conflict and hostility would lift. But I could never take the offer seriously, knowing what I knew about the organization. Jesus was the one who had given his life for the sins of the world. He was Savior, Lord, and God Almighty—not a good teacher on the same level as the leaders of other world religions or cults. No, the issue was not whether I would ever accept such an invitation; the issue was whether I should just say *no thank you!* or make an effort to explain myself. I decided to write a letter, a very gentle letter, and explain myself.

And that's how the fat hit the pan. There was an uproar in the organization. My letter was copied scores of times and distributed all over the map, and immediately families that belonged to the organization began to leave the church in the hope that the lost finances and diminishing numbers would kill us. It was pretty grim. Yet all the time the founding pastor and members of the organization had been grinding their teeth at my messages, new people had been coming to the church — older people, young families, persons seeking something more than religion. Many had given their lives to Christ, not to the organization, and this changed the entire church dynamic in little more than half a year. It was these folks who supported the ministry of my wife and me, and it was they who hung in there as the going got tough.

I distinctly remember standing up to preach one Sunday and noticing all the empty seats. *Lord*, I prayed, *my wife and I have taken this stand for your gospel's sake and for your name. Please fill the empty seats with those who want to follow you.* And over the next few weeks and months the Lord did just that. He completely changed the face of that church.

But the whole thing took its toll, and after two years I was exhausted and came to the conclusion that another minister would be able to carry on much better than I could. So I resigned. While I was on vacation, the founding minister, who had disappeared for a while, suddenly showed up again and worked at ingratiating himself with old members and new members. Members of my leadership team, many of whom had joined the church after my wife and I arrived, approached me and asked if I would consider a leave of absence instead — in the hope that the Lord would heal and rejuvenate me. So my wife and I prayed about it, and I withdrew my resignation. An interim minister was brought in who believed in the gospel of Jesus Christ, the founding pastor was stymied, and I stayed home and fought to get well.

I really had pushed it during those difficult months and wound up contracting a condition similar to mononucleosis. Some days I could scarcely move my limbs to get out of bed. I had never been weaker in my life. While my wife nursed by day, I took my dogs, Yukon and Nahanni—lively dogs that simply had to be walked (and run) unless we wanted growling, snapping animals—and went into the mountains across the highway.

Those first weeks of my leave of absence, I could hardly move uphill without collapsing to rest. The dogs must have wondered why I was so slow, but they stuck with me nevertheless. I was constantly seeking out boulders and stumps to sit on. As time went by, I could climb higher and higher up the old trails and overgrown logging roads. Soon we were walking beside and across the many alpine streams and rivers that cut their way through the green wilderness. And the month came when I no longer felt tired as we hiked higher and higher into the mountains.

My wife had prayed I would get off my sickbed. My dogs *made* me get off my sickbed. Without the help of all three, I would never have made it. God used them to save my life.

After four months, I returned to the church. No doubt the organization was dismayed. I had read enough of their literature to know that they had not only spoken against me in their meetings but probably enacted rituals against me as well. Yet there I stood, more energetic than ever. They had run into a power greater than their own. Jesus Christ, the divine Son of God, had restored my health and my soul.

Of course, the thing is, when you go through a confrontation like this, at first you are praying against what your enemy is trying to do. In a little while, God has you praying for your enemy. Your body is healed, but so is your heart. I did not have much common ground with the men and women who had stood against my wife and me, nor did I like what they were trying to do, but I did not wind up hating them either. You simply cannot pray for people to be blessed and transformed and hate them at the same time—Jesus will not let you.

We stayed for five years at the church and saw many people saved and baptized in the years to come. Yes, there were other battles and difficulties, as there inevitably are in ministry, but we saw a great deal more of what was good than what was evil. And God capped it with an amazing conclusion—a season of great spiritual renewal and refreshing that changed dozens of lives at the church and made all the suffering my wife and I had gone through seem like one short, dark night in comparison to a longer and brighter day.

We had been in the desert for a season. But God did not leave us there. And we emerged, filled with faith and strength as he poured his waters of life on us.

THREE

Sometimes the challenges we take on and the sufferings we struggle with can wear us down. They may go on for a long time, and we may not see any of the results we would call good for even longer. This can take us into a desert experience in which our faith feels dried up, stunted, practically lifeless.

The first generation that left captivity in Egypt knew something about this sort of desert experience. Despite all the miracles they had seen, despite the ways in which God provided for them every step of the journey, they not only complained the whole time; when they had a chance to enter the Promised Land, they were afraid. They preferred to stay in the desert rather than cross the Jordan into a completely new situation. Their children went over the Jordan years later, but they didn't.

The prophet Elijah knew something about the desert experience. He was fleeing from Queen Jezebel's vengeance, but he was also fleeing from his calling as a prophet. He was tired and fed up, and in essence he went out to the desert to die. But God gave him food and water, and they met on the mountain where Moses had received the Ten Commandments.

David knew something about the desert experience. As a young man, he had to flee from Saul, the king of Israel, who was jealous of David and wanted him dead. David spent years in the wilderness. And he had to do the desert experience again when he himself was king—as a consequence of his adultery with Bathsheba and the murder of her husband, Uriah. His son Absalom rebelled against him and took his throne. David fled into the desert. Eventually his throne was restored to him—but at the cost of Absalom's life.

In each case, the desert experience turned into a rejuvenation experience, yet there was danger and pain involved, as well as restoration.

The parents did not enter the Promised Land. They didn't want to, but God rejuvenated his people and his plan by bringing their children across the Jordan instead.

Elijah would have died in the desert, but God brought angels into the situation and rejuvenated the prophet not only with food and water but also by setting up a personal encounter with him on a mountaintop. He rejuvenated Elijah's prophetic calling by taking him into heaven in a whirlwind and leaving Elisha to carry on in Elijah's place.

When Saul was killed in battle, the throne of Israel and David's own calling were both rejuvenated when the crown was placed on David's head. When Absalom was killed in battle, the throne of Israel and David's own calling were again rejuvenated when the crown was replaced on David's head. Yet in both cases, David experienced not only restoration but the danger that came before the restoration. And he experienced grief as well—he wept at Saul's death as well as at the death of his son Absalom.

"There is danger when the rains come," the woman who experienced the thunder season of Arizona had told me, "but most of all, the rivers of the desert bring life—and it's always a sudden rush and always a great surprise."

FOUR

We were moving along at a good clip down the highway, returning from a short Christmas vacation with family. A turn was coming up—I hadn't decided whether to take it or not. My wife was leaving it up to me since it was more my call than hers.

I was going through my own desert experience in a church I was pastoring. I felt so depleted and worn-out inside I didn't know if it was worth it to even attempt to step behind the pulpit again or to sit down with my leadership group and pray for my ministry to the church families.

The church had been a challenge from the beginning, but, thanks to God, my wife and I had met that challenge and seen the waters part. But now, over on the other side, just as Joshua and Israel did, we found fresh conflict and difficulty. At some point, it began to feel overwhelming. My emotional, physical, and spiritual health deteriorated. The Bible seemed dry as I read it. My prayers lodged in my throat. I had lost my vision of service to God and ministry to others and any sense of anticipation of what God might do next to bless and invigorate his people. "A desert is a place without expectation," states South African writer Nadine Gordimer.

The right thing, it seemed to me, was to quit. To do so

might not heal me, but it would allow the church to find a pastor with fresh energy and zeal. And the absence of stress would help me eat and sleep better and maybe even laugh wholeheartedly again.

The exit ramp was almost on us. It led to a Christian prayer and retreat center. They had promised an open door if we wanted to pull in and stay a week, a month, as long as it took. I could talk things over with my church leadership from there. We knew the staff at the center. They loved the Lord and loved people. My wife and I were not strangers to them. We knew we would be in good hands if I chose to click on my turn signal and move to the right.

The time came. I can still remember my wife's eyes fixed on me. I glanced at the turning lane just over her shoulder, hesitated a moment, and kept going.

There was no big sigh of relief because a decision had been made. For one thing, I kept second-guessing myself for the next two hours, and my wife kept responding, "You can always turn around and go back." For another, it wasn't as if choosing to go on made me feel excited about life. I was heading into a spiritual battle zone. There was nothing to look forward to.

It was a wild and windy night when we parked the car in our driveway. Our home was close to a saltwater bay and the ocean, so we decided to head down to the beach. Trees tossed and branches flapped, and once we got to the beach, we began to walk, surf pounding white in the dark. We were holding hands but not saying much. The shriek of the wind and roaring of the water made it difficult to hear anyway.

We came to a point where rock and sand jutted out into the bay. The sea seethed and heaved. Suddenly we were heading right into the smash of the breakers, hand in hand, not caring about our shoes or socks or jeans. Waves smacked into our legs and spray broke over our shirts and jackets. It didn't matter. Wind tearing at our faces, we began to sing Rich Mullins's "Our God Is an Awesome God" at the top of our lungs.

We were loud, and we kept singing the chorus over and over again, but I doubt anyone heard us except God. The storm was at its height. Salt water was smacking and cracking and exploding into the rocks, and the wind was howling right over our heads. Still, we sang. It was an act of worship, but it was also an act of defiance. We worshiped Christ with our storm music, but we defied the devil. God was greater than he was, and no matter what he threw at us, we were counting on God to see us through. With the storm still raging, we eventually returned to the house, soaked and cold and exhilarated. I slept the better for it.

The battles we anticipated—and those we hadn't—came at us in a fury over the next weeks and months. Somehow, by God's grace, we hung in there. I remember being surprised at a new stamina and vitality I hadn't felt in a long time. The Bible leaped to life in my hands; prayer gleamed like starlight through a long night. Rivers were streaming through the dry riverbeds of my heart, and I was coming to life again. God had planted an oasis in my soul.

When I look back at that time in our lives, I realize that if I had gotten off at that exit, my wife and I would have missed out on some of the greatest blessings in our lives. The baptisms we celebrated from that time of ministry, the persons who came to Christ, the Christian community that developed in that church—all of this happened *after* that night we sang into the storm. If we'd gone to the prayer center and called it quits, we would never have discovered how God can turn a desert experience into a renewal experience. Yes, God would have been at work in our lives at the prayer center too, no question, and we would have seen marvelous things spring to life there as well. Yet somehow sticking to the church we'd felt called to and crying out for God to *restore our lives like streams in the Negev* showed us a wonder and beauty and power from the hand of God we had never known before.

As tough as our early days were, and the desert experience that came out of it, if I had to do it over, I would not alter a thing. The desert brought us to a place where the Lord had to fill the dry riverbeds with his grace and love, and once he did, it was not only us who lived again; others came to Christ and lived as well, and we saw the glory of God.

FIVE

Jesus knew a desert experience. More than one, I suppose, for Gethsemane and the crucifixion were certainly deserts that were eventually seamed with silver rivers of life at his resurrection. But in only one story were real sand, desert heat, and wilderness involved — an emptiness that was not empty. "To say nothing is out here is incorrect," writes American author William Least Heat Moon, "to say the desert is stingy with everything except space and light, stone and earth, is closer to the truth."

Jesus had not refused to obey God, as Israel had. He was not fed up and hoping to end his ministry and his life, like Elijah was. He was not being pursued by a bitter king or by retribution for past sins of adultery and murder, as was true for David. The Holy Spirit led Jesus into the desert for a time of testing that was critical for him. And he did not emerge a broken man. Though going without food for forty days and feeling hungry and tired by the end, he came out of the desert like a lion, fully rejuvenated, focused, and ready to begin his ministry as the Son of God and the Son of Man. "Jesus returned to Galilee," Luke writes after the desert experience is finished, "in the power of the Spirit" (Luke 4:14).

There are a number of Bible passages that speak to this spiritual phenomenon, a dry and difficult desert season for a person's faith that ends with a sudden outpouring of life. One song recalls the return of Israel from exile and how sweet that moment was. They ask God to do it again: "Restore our fortunes, O LORD, like streams in the Negev" (Psalm 126:4). To bring out the meaning more fully, we might say something like this: "Restore our lives, Lord, as you restore torrents of water to the empty riverbeds in the desert." The songwriter is asking God to bring that rush of new life only his Spirit can give and rejuvenate his people in the same way rain fills the riverbeds and brings vitality to the plants, animals, and people of the desert.

A prophecy in Isaiah that looks forward to Israel's return from exile (and is also seen as predicting the coming of the Messiah) picks up on this same idea. It compares Israel's return and the Messiah's arrival to the return of life to an arid desert:

> *The desert and the parched land will be glad;*
> *the wilderness will rejoice and blossom.*
> *Like the crocus, it will burst into bloom;*
> *it will rejoice greatly and shout for joy....*
>
> *Then will the eyes of the blind be opened*
> *and the ears of the deaf unstopped.*
> *Then will the lame leap like a deer,*
> *and the mute tongue shout for joy.*
> *Water will gush forth in the wilderness*
> *and streams in the desert.*
> *The burning sand will become a pool,*
> *the thirsty ground bubbling springs.*
> *In the haunts where jackals once lay,*
> *grass and reeds and papyrus will grow.*
>
> Isaiah 35:1–2, 5–7

Isaiah tells us of a spiritual life — one that has been blind and deaf and speechless, stunted and unable to grow or move, parched and thirsty — that is completely rejuvenated by a new intimacy with God and a fresh openness to his will. The wadis and arroyos of the heart flow again with his Spirit. All kinds of persons bloom in their relationship with God and others where before there had been little sign of life or fruit at all.

In another passage, God declares that he will not forget those who are undergoing a desert experience but will restore them:

> *The poor and needy search for water,*
> *but there is none;*
> *their tongues are parched with thirst.*
> *But I the Lord will answer them;*
> *I, the God of Israel, will not forsake them.*
> *I will make rivers flow on barren heights,*
> *and springs within the valleys.*
> *I will turn the desert into pools of water,*
> *and the parched ground into springs.*
> *I will put in the desert*
> *the cedar and the acacia, the myrtle and the olive.*
> *I will set pines in the wasteland,*
> *the fir and the cypress together,*
> *so that people may see and know,*
> *may consider and understand,*
> *that the hand of the Lord has done this,*
> *that the Holy One of Israel has created it.*
>
> Isaiah 41:17 – 20

Not only will the dusty riverbeds run with new life in bone-dry hearts; God also promises to plant all sorts of trees in the spirits of the parched and the struggling. If you've seen any of these trees in the world around us—pines, cypress, cedar, fir, olive, myrtle, and acacia—you know how wonderful they are. Imagine them growing in a place that has no reliable source of water. They would die. Yet God says he'll plant this sort of majestic, fruitful life in the midst of a soul that has seen hard times and may be close to exhausting any supply of faith and hope. How is it possible for this to happen? Only if God rejuvenates the soul so that all kinds of wholeness and holiness that could not sink roots before is now in a heart where they can thrive.

And he revitalizes these lives in such a way that they know *God* is doing it, not anything or anyone else. They will not be able to claim that money did it, or a sudden romance, or fame, or a pill. The healing and restoration is so profound, so amazing, so difficult to comprehend that it cannot be grasped in any other way except to come right out and admit it must be a miracle from the hand of God.

God has more to say about this:

> *"Forget the former things;*
> *do not dwell on the past.*
> *See, I am doing a new thing!*
> *Now it springs up; do you not perceive it?*
> *I am making a way in the desert*
> *and streams in the wasteland.*
> *The wild animals honor me,*
> *the jackals and the owls,*

> *because I provide water in the desert*
>   *and streams in the wasteland,*
> *to give drink to my people, my chosen,*
>   *the people I formed for myself*
>   *that they may proclaim my praise."*
>
> Isaiah 43:18–21

In the hard places, in the desert places, God makes the rivers run so that his people have what they need to drink. This gives his people both the strength and the faith to honor and praise him. This image of the desert flowing with water and God's people being refreshed is even included in the most famous song in the entire Bible:

> *The LORD is my shepherd, I lack nothing.*
>   *He makes me lie down in green pastures,*
> *he leads me beside quiet waters,*
>   *he refreshes my soul.*
>
> Psalm 23:1–3 TNIV

Before his times of stress and struggle with Saul and Absalom, David had the desert experience of protecting his flock from predators, watching over them day and night, always on the lookout for good pasture and fresh water. His whole song is about God doing what David did with the livestock under his care—protecting, feeding, nurturing. But the image he gives us at the beginning is one of finding sustenance when we feel weak and powerless, when we have little enthusiasm for things of the spirit and still less focus and faith to follow through on what we say we believe, when the soul is depleted. So like all the other passages that picture God putting water in the rough and dry places where we do not expect to see it, David's thoughts revolve around what it takes to restore spiritual life to a person — quiet, peace, the green pastures of food and growth, and water. Without water there can be quiet, but there cannot be the green of things that thrive or the water that brings back zest and a future. And the quiet that exists with good water at hand is different from the sort of quiet that exists without it. *God is the water*, David asserts, *that refreshes my dry soul.*

Jesus has many titles, and we have many different ways of describing who he is and what he does. He is the Bread of Life; the Prince of Peace; the Way and the Truth and the Life. He is also the one who gives us living water, the kind that breaks the grip of the desert experience and reinvigorates our souls. Ultimately, Jesus is the source of the water that enlivens the spiritual wastelands; in fact, he is the water itself. He is the winter and summer rains that end the heart's aridity; it is he who makes the deserts of our lives burst forth with new beauty and new beginnings.

So it is important, from time to time, to remember him as the river in the desert who replenishes all the creeks and streams and waterways of our relationship with God. We need to call out to him when we are in those dry, thirsty lands of our lives, when we lack the water that is the Spirit of God: " 'Let anyone who is thirsty come to me and drink. Whoever believes in me, as Scripture has said, rivers of living water will flow from within them.' By this he meant the Spirit" (John 7:37 – 39 TNIV).

SIX

At one time, my wife and I pastored in a resort area. As a result, we often saw visitors from all over the world in our congregation on Sunday mornings. Bob and his wife, Sara, were two such visitors. They sat quietly in their seats, though I remember Bob's gaze was intense and his tanned face vibrant with energy and goodwill. When I asked them to introduce themselves, they told us they were missionaries who had been working among the Bedouin of the Middle East for most of their lives.

Not your normal Sunday visitors, even for a resort area church. So I asked them to share for a few minutes. Someone must have asked about worship music, because Sara began to sing a chorus in Arabic. It was shrill and high-pitched, and when Sara suddenly trilled sharply with her tongue, Bob exploded, jumping up and down and crying, "Hi! Hi! Hi! Hi!" The congregation was both astonished and delighted by their youthful enthusiasm.

Then Bob began to speak. He was soft-spoken, yet his words were even more astonishing than the song. I remember the words well, because later that day I wrote down the gist of what he said:

> In twenty-five years we never saw one Bedouin tribesman come to Jesus Christ. In twenty-five years not even one came to our tent to ask us more about Jesus. With

their camels beside them, they listened to our messages at the different oases, and then they went on with their lives. In twenty-five years we counseled no one and baptized no one. For twenty-five years we sang our songs to God alone. But to God we sang them, not to thin air, for we saw him face-to-face, and each day his glory was like a pillar of fire in the Arabian sky. We ate and drank with God. We slept under God's grace. We woke drenched in his light and in anticipation of more of his love. We were Abraham. We were Moses. We were Paul. We were in a splendid desert, and there was no clutter, no traffic. No one had a cell phone; no one had a schedule. There was so much room for God. And in the twenty-eighth year we baptized our first tribesman, Ali. What a glory! What a life! Oh God, I thank you, our living God, our blazing God, our mighty God who sees and saves!

Not your typical Sunday morning message, was it?

My wife and I and several others had lunch with them. Later Bob and I enjoyed several minutes alone.

"How did the mission board handle all this?" I asked.

Bob smiled. "After ten years they wanted us out because, you know, the mission was not productive. But we asked to stay on, and they agreed to five more years. Once we'd reached the fifteen-year mark without even one convert, they definitely wanted us out. But we kept asking to stay on. So fifteen became twenty and twenty became twenty-five without one Bedouin coming to Christ. Some of the board members had actually died since we started our mission, and a few of the others who were still there wanted to pull their hair out—or ours, I'm not sure which." Bob paused to laugh. There was absolutely no bitterness in him. "But the new members wanted to see what God would do, so we were allowed to stay on. It was a big day for them and us when Ali gave his life to Christ. Big day for heaven too."

"Was that it? Did anyone else come to Christ?"

"Oh, yes. Ali was the first. A couple of years later, there were a few more. By the time thirty years rolled around, we had almost a dozen. It was incredible. It actually got crowded in the tent." He winked.

"And now what?"

"Now they are in the hands of their own leaders who have followed Christ. And in the hands of God."

"Didn't you ever get discouraged, not just with what was going on in the desert but by your struggles with the mission board too?"

Bob nodded. "It was hard, very hard. Sara and I would pray and fast and lose sleep over it. And then there was the night I stepped out of our tent at three in the morning, and I saw God in everything that was going on—every difficulty, every obstacle, every hope, every dream we had for the Bedouin. It transformed the night sky, and it transformed my heart. How can you ever live life half full again once you've seen the glory of God?"

His soul gleamed through his dark skin like a sun.

When we parted, he shook my hand and hugged me: "If you ever need a camel or an oasis or a desert, call me."

I remembered the Bedouin from my trips up and down the Sinai Peninsula. Yes, there were camels, and black goatskin tents, and TV antennae sticking out of the tents. They dressed in robes, turbans, heavy overcoats, and boots in the desert heat, strange dark garb compared to the rest of us, who wore shorts and sandals and little else. I thought of them praying and reading about Jesus together, and it suddenly seemed like a better world than the one I had woken up to.

Bob and Sara had known the heat and dust and chilly dawns of the physical desert. They had also known the desert of working at something they believed in for half a lifetime without seeing anything measurable coming out of it. And they had experienced the desert of having a support team start to lose faith in you and in what you were hoping to accomplish. Yet, in the end, in God's timing, which is often not ours, rivers flowed in the wadis and children of the desert became children of God.

When we think about our struggle with impatience and our battle to remember in the face of disappointments that God's ways are not our ways, hearing Bob and Sara's story puts things in perspective. They saw the glory of God before they saw even one person believe in the gospel message. They experienced the renewing vigor of the Holy Spirit long before their mission or life journey was ever complete. We often think of God as rewarding our best efforts, but in so many cases what we receive instead is a touch of his grace.

SEVEN

"My people have committed two sins," God reveals prior to the fall of Jerusalem. "They have forsaken me, the spring of living water, and have dug their own cisterns, broken cisterns that cannot hold water" (Jeremiah 2:13).

Often a desert experience seems to be another way of talking about suffering. I think the main difference is that most desert experiences center around a loss of faith—or a struggle or weakening of faith—whereas any number of people can go through suffering and not lose sight of God at all. Indeed, for some, suffering may bring them closer to God, not pry them apart.

When people turn their backs on God or are too worn-out to care anymore, when they look to other things to take God's place, they cut themselves off from the source, the Lord himself, the spring of living water. Israel did it when they refused to enter the Promised Land. They did not trust God to take care of them, and that was that. For forty years they were in a literal and a spiritual desert until the generation that had lost its faith passed away. Elijah had lost faith too, not in God's existence, but in God's plan for him and for Israel. When David committed both murder and adultery, he was turning his back on God and God's ways.

The desert experience also occurs when others turn their

backs on God and afflict us. Saul did this to David. Paul had the experience of false brothers turning on him, as well as true brothers who had lost their focus on Christ. Even Jesus felt the pain of having his disciples turn their backs on him when he spoke of them eating his body and drinking his blood. And he felt the sting of having a disciple betray him to the men who wanted to kill him.

Paul lists hardships he endured because of the gospel (2 Corinthians 11:22–28) — five times given the thirty-nine lashes, three times beaten with rods, one time pelted with stones, three times shipwrecked, in danger from bandits and Jews and Greeks and Romans and false believers. We see that some of these experiences were difficulties and sufferings that, as far as we know, did not involve wrestling with his faith; some of these experiences, judging from what we know about human nature and the price of following Christ, may very well have been. "As servants of God," he also wrote, "we commend ourselves in every way: in great endurance; in troubles, hardships and distresses; ... dying, and yet we live on; beaten, and yet not killed; sorrowful, yet always rejoicing" (2 Corinthians 6:4, 9–10).

Some desert experiences involve our loss of faith or the loss of faith of others who have influence over our lives. Some happen because we have grown weak spiritually. Some are simply thrust on us according to the ways of God. Some come because following Christ has placed us between a rock and a hard place.

Jesus did not sin or lose faith in the Father, yet he wrestled with going to the cross to the point where several times he asked that he be spared crucifixion. That was a desert for him, and there was no real turnaround in the situation until Sunday morning.

When Jesus shouted from the cross, torn with physical, psychological, and spiritual pain, *"Eli, Eli, lema sabachthani?"* ("My God, my God, why have you forsaken me?" Matthew 27:46 TNIV), he was feeling cut off from the Father—and that also was a desert for him, as it would be for any of us.

Paul often comes across as invincible, yet when he was on the long voyage to Rome, in danger of shipwreck, God felt he needed some encouragement: "Last night an angel of the God whose I am and whom I serve stood beside me and said, 'Do not be afraid, Paul. You must stand trial before Caesar; and God has graciously given you the lives of all who sail with you'" (Acts 27:23–24). God doesn't send angels unless there is a reason. Paul was struggling with what was going to happen. It was a long desert experience to get to Rome, and much of it was spent in strange places or on the open sea. The angel's message strengthened his faith: "I have faith in God that it will happen just as he told me" (Acts 27:25).

Peter went through a desert experience when he denied knowing Jesus. It was a bitter weekend for him. A desert. There was restoration by the Sea of Galilee after the resurrection, but not before. A further rejuvenation occurred at Pentecost, when the Spirit fell and he preached with power and conviction.

What would we call what all the disciples went through the weekend Jesus was in the grave? Did any of the men expect to see him rise from the dead on that Sunday morning? Any of the women? His mother? Mary Magdalene? It was a dry and empty stretch of time for each of them. None of them believed they would see Jesus alive again. But the life-giving waters of the Spirit gushed through their hearts when they saw he really had risen, and it restored their faith.

Go through the Bible from Genesis to Revelation, and you'll find many more stories in which a desert experience ends with a wonderful restoration due to the love and power of God. Think of Ruth and of Esther. Of Ezra and Nehemiah. Of Job. Of Daniel. Of Peter and Paul and Jesus and Mary and other people we've already spoken about. It's important not to give up hope when we experience a drought of the spirit. It's important to remember that many others have gone through the same thing and emerged on the other side exhilarated and closer to God.

> *I will pour water on the thirsty land,*
>   *and streams on the dry ground;*
> *I will pour out my Spirit on your offspring,*
>   *and my blessing on your descendants.*
> *They will spring up like grass in a meadow,*
>   *like poplar trees by flowing streams.*
> *One will say, "I belong to the LORD";*
>   *another will call himself by the name of Jacob;*
> *still another will write on his hand, 'The LORD's,'*
>   *and will take the name Israel.*

Isaiah 44:3–5

I have been in the deserts of America, Afghanistan, Egypt, Iran, and Israel. I love the desert. I love the chill of the night and the stars as bright as comets. I love the sun of the day and the shimmering heat waves that lift from the sand. I love the purple and orange mountains and rocks. I love the distance and the blue and platinum of the afternoon sky.

Yet I have come after hours of travel in the desert to an oasis and fresh water and thanked God. I have come as a soldier, carrying only two full canteens for an entire day of marching, to a place of trees and tents and trucks that carried enough water to fill the mouths of an army and thanked God. I have been in such heat that I daydreamed all day of the coolness at sunset, and when it came, I sat and drank and thanked God.

I know how beautiful the desert is. I also know that without water it is a death trap. With water, on the other hand, it is a place of surprising life. As the French aviator and writer Antoine de Saint-Exupery puts it, "What makes the desert beautiful is that somewhere it hides a well."

The desert experience Christians go through would mean nothing if those experiences did not end with the soul's restoration. The Lord teaches us valuable lessons in the desert, and we go through significant tests that can make us stronger — look at Christ's own experience, or Elijah's, or David's. It was in the desert that Moses encountered the burning bush; it was in the desert that he received the Ten Commandments. Yet none of them would tell you that their desert journey meant anything apart from God. "Why do I live in the desert?" wrote American author Edward Abbey. "Because the desert is the locus Dei" — the place of God. If we do not meet God in our spiritual desert, we die, because God is the spring of living water.

There was a time that drought struck the land where I lived.

Everyone was concerned—not just the ranchers and farmers. I often ran my dogs out by the reservoir, which was also a recreational lake. Week by week, month by month, I watched the blue water shrink farther back from the shore. That winter and summer, we could walk right down into the bowels of the reservoir and see the roadways that had been used by earthmoving equipment and discover gear that had been left behind and under the water for many years. It was a strange sensation to be able to go down almost to the bottom of the lake. The land needed more rain and snow, but very little came our way.

I began to go through my own drought. It affected almost every area of my life. I stood by the vanishing reservoir with a friend I had confided in. The sun blazed over the landscape. The grass was brown, the soil hard and cracked. Breezes blew dust high into the air. Everything looked dried-up and lifeless—a desert where once there had been bright water, children swimming, white pelicans swooping, deer grazing in the tall green grasses. As we looked at the blowing dirt, my friend glanced at me: "This is how you feel, isn't it?"

Now, no one in his right mind would want the lake to stay that way or his life to stay that way. While people prayed and hoped for rain, I prayed along with them—and I also prayed for my own spiritual riverbeds and reservoir to become filled. Maybe I was learning some hard and important lessons from my desert experience, but if God and I didn't connect soon, there wouldn't be much of me left to live out what I had gained from my struggles.

Almost an hour south of the dying reservoir was a turnoff

that led into the mountains and trees. Here were places to camp, but the setting was primitive, so not many people stopped by. A river curled slowly through the campground, flowing out of the mountains, a translucent emerald green. There was a sandy shore where you could sit and just watch it move—placid, sure, perpetual. Farther downstream were rapids. All around were purple mountains and long fields.

I often went there with my family, but I would also go alone. My dogs and I would go for long hikes in the wilderness, a Bowie strapped to my side. As the dogs swam and drank in the cool green waters, I would watch their pleasure and smile. One of my favorite birds, the great blue heron, often flew overhead or waded nearby. At my tent I might sit on a stump and whittle or read a book or the Bible. I did not have any answers for the bleakness in my heart, but the rhythm of the river and the mountains and the stars brought me peace.

If you've ever been in the mountains for any amount of time you know what a thunderstorm is like when it passes through—the roar, the tearing of air and earth, the scorching white flashes of lightning. Storm after storm blasted and crashed through my camp that summer—smashing rain for ten minutes, then blue sky and heat; another system with clouds piled higher than the highest peaks and looking like the fists and biceps of giants, then more wind and rain and deep, dark, angry rumbles and growls and bursts of rage. I sat in the Jeep, my dogs huddled beside me, and watched every show that came our way. When they ended, we would emerge into heat and steam and a world shining like nickels.

At such moments, I began to pray: *Lord, make it like this inside me—new and bright and growing. Put rivers in me and blue sky and mountains capped with snow. Put your constellations in me and your rain clouds and your strong winds. Live in me again, my God. Thrive in me, and fill me to the brim with your Spirit.*

Have I found beauty in the desert and in the desert experience of the soul? Yes, I have. Do I want to stay in those deserts without water or without God? No, I don't. So when the day came—and it did come—when snows and rains replenished the reservoir, I was glad, and when the day came that God put rivers in me again, and rainfall, and sunlight and mountains and stars, I laughed and danced and praised his name.

For the Lord is about rejuvenation. He is about restoration. He is about healing and blessing and hope, and I would never wish to stay in any state of mind or heart in which I feel less of him or less of his power or majesty or compassion. He is life—life the color of rich summer—and I want that life and color and summer in me without limit and without hindrance. Better one day in his world than a thousand elsewhere. The sweetest distractions on earth are nothing compared to his vibrancy and deep-down goodness and rock-solid love. I want him unleashed to be all he is and all he wants to be in me, and I want that life experience to be unending and unstoppable.

> The Spirit and the bride say, "Come!" And let those who hear say, "Come!" Let those who are thirsty come; and let all who wish take the free gift of the water of life.
>
> Revelation 22:17 TNIV

PART FOUR

THE JORDAN RIVER

The WATERS *of* NEW LIFE

*Jesus came from Nazareth in Galilee
and was baptized by John in the Jordan.*
Mark 1:9

ONE

My two dogs and I had passed this way many times before and never stopped. There was no reason to. The logging road we were on stretched invitingly into the long depths of the forest and could take us places where few people had been for fifty, sixty, or even one hundred years. We had discovered ancient wooden railroad trestles spanning forgotten gorges. We had unearthed old campsites littered with blackened tin cans, thick square-bottomed glass bottles, and large, rusting saw blades curled in on themselves, all left behind by the lumberjacks of another era. There were black bears and elk, and one time we picked up the overpowering scent of a cougar. Many trees had grown high since the loggers had left, and I often stood in awe among the green pillars that dwarfed me and shut out the sun. There was simply too much to see the further we went along the road. Why stop to take a scrawny little path that appeared to peter out in the underbrush less than fifty feet away?

But my dogs, Yukon and Nahanni, were keen that day to branch off on the derelict path. I hesitated, the overgrown logging road promising familiar beauty and adventure. Then I relented.

"All right, old dogs," I said. "We'll take this path just this once, but I don't think it's going to lead us anywhere."

They rushed on ahead, noses to the ground. The trail was no more than a pencil line hastily sketched on the earth, a line that was often obscured by grass and weed and brush. Still, there remained something to follow, so I carried on. After about five minutes, the trail broadened slightly and, to my surprise, became more of an actual path — not heavily used, and certainly not used much by humans, but it had seen wear that was not decades old. The three of us went along for about ten minutes, and I began to wonder where we would end up. Where was this odd little trail taking us? Then I heard the roar of water.

I glimpsed the flash of silver through the trees to my right. In another couple of minutes the path stopped at a cliff, the trees opened up, and a waterfall poured over rock and stone into a pond far below. The pond was emerald, the cataract white and jade. Spray made prisms that scattered drops of violet and crimson; a thousand sword ferns stirred at the rim of the water. I couldn't have been more surprised if I had stumbled on the Garden of Eden.

The cliff was steep, but it was dirt and mud, not rock, and the three of us slid and scrambled down. Yukon and Nahanni began to thirstily gulp the fresh water. I bent and splashed some to my face. It was like being transported into another dimension, as if I'd somehow walked through a wrinkle in space and time and wound up in Maui or Fiji or Barbados. The sword fern gave the place a tropical feel. Who would have thought a path that began so poorly would take me to a place that radiated so much life and beauty, hidden deep in the forest, unseen by most?

I called it The Lagoon. And I brought the next group of

people who wanted to be baptized to that waterfall and pond. It was a rough ride on the old logging road, followed by a stiff hike down that normal-looking trail. At the falls, a number of older people from the church remained standing and watching at the top of the cliff, while the rest of us made our way down. We even brought white baptismal robes. Sunlight flickered off the cascading water and off the robes and off the ripples that were stirred up as we waded into the pond and close to the silver turbulence. In the name of Jesus, in that place I baptized four men and women. Surrounded by beauty in an unlikely spot, immersed in that beauty, saying yes again to the Maker of beauty who had placed his own beauty deep within the forest of each of their hearts, I stood wet and happy as each person returned to towels and hugs on the shore. We sang, and our voices sang back to us among the waters and the green.

There could be no better place to baptize a Christian, I thought as we worshiped. No better place at all than this. It was all the zest and radiance of God and the new life in Christ in one small corner of the earth. It was perfect. The only place that could be more perfect was the river where Jesus himself was baptized — the Jordan.

TWO

For a Christian there is no more famous body of water in the Bible than the Jordan River. We have written about it, sung hymns and spirituals about it, painted our baptismal tanks to look like it—palm trees, sand, blue sky. When Christians visit Israel, many are baptized a second time in the Jordan—all because Jesus himself was baptized by John in that river.

Of course, our reasons for being baptized are different from the reason Jesus went to the Jordan. He wasn't there to repent, to express remorse for sinful behavior, and to put an end to wrong ways of living, like the others John was baptizing. He obviously wasn't there to express his commitment to Christ, either, as Christians do when they are baptized. John himself was confused that Jesus showed up at the Jordan at all: *Look, I need you to baptize me and yet you want me, a sinful human, to baptize you?* It didn't make any sense.

But Jesus was going through his own act of commitment at the Jordan. "Let it be so now," he responded to John. "It is proper for us to do this to fulfill all righteousness" (Matthew 3:15). Or to put it another way, "Do it. God's work, putting things right all these centuries, is coming together right now in this baptism" (MSG). Jesus' baptism was an act of dedication to God the Father and an act of consecration to God's ways. In the same way that we identify totally with Christ at our baptism, Jesus was identifying totally with God the Father at his. And the Father commended the baptism. The Holy Spirit lighted on Jesus in the form of a dove. The Father spoke aloud his words of approval: "This is my Son, whom I love; with him I am well pleased" (Matthew 3:17).

Later on, John the Baptist would remember the day and the moment vividly: "I saw the Spirit come down from heaven as a dove and remain on him" (John 1:32). He recalls that he wouldn't have known who Jesus truly was—even though Jesus was his cousin through the relationship between Mary and Elizabeth —except for the fact that God had told him the person on whom the Spirit came and rested, white wings blurring to slow the descent, was the one who would baptize with the Holy Spirit (verse 33). "I myself did not know him," John said, "but the reason I came baptizing with water was that he might be revealed to Israel" (verse 31).

So it was an enormous moment. No doubt God used all of John's preaching and baptizing at the Jordan for good, but John himself admits the main reason he did what he did was so that Jesus might be seen for who he was. The baptism was the beginning. Previously, Jesus had lived a simple and private and unknown life. Now he would become a public figure. There would be crowds, controversy, authoritative words, powerful healings, people who loved him and people who hated him. The baptism at the Jordan was the start of his second life.

It's no different for us. We come to the point where we believe in Jesus, and it's a new life and a new world—we are born a second time. Our baptism as believers is an outward sign or symbol of this. It's our new start. We are being released to be all God meant for us to be. No wonder many Christians want to link up with the fresh start Jesus made and have a second baptism in the Jordan. It's a place of great significance for the believer who wants to follow Jesus wholeheartedly.

I have lived in Israel, but I never made the trip to be baptized a second time in the Jordan River. Yet I can see why people would do it. It's a way of connecting with Jesus. And a Christian's baptism is all about connecting with Jesus—heart, mind, soul, and strength—just as Jesus' baptism was about connecting with the Father.

For some it can be a very ordinary event. The heavens don't open. There are no doves or voices. They may not feel any sort of spiritual or emotional high, but it's the right thing to do, and so they do it. The ordinariness doesn't make baptism have any less impact on their souls; their request is not empty, for Christ will still work powerfully in their lives. Sometimes a spiritual event goes through us like wildfire; sometimes it's no more than a breeze—still real, still holy, still life changing, but taking place quietly in our souls. Remember Elijah in the cave in the desert waiting for God? God wasn't in the fire or the wind or the earthquake, but in a "gentle whisper" (1 Kings 19:12).

I baptized my son in a creek rife with rainbow trout; I baptized my daughter in the Atlantic Ocean at sunset. I have baptized people in white water so ferocious that if I had let go they would have been swept away. The Pacific Ocean at dawn, strong prairie rivers, ice-cold mountain lakes with snow-capped peaks and glaciers as a backdrop—all of them have been extraordinary events in often extraordinary places. Yes, sometimes I've baptized indoors too, and once I used a hot tub in a family's front yard. Often my wife has joined me in baptizing believers. None of these events, whether in a sea or river or mountain lake, have meant any less or any more than any other baptism.

Yet my own baptism, on the surface, appears like one of the most ordinary of all. It was a cold Easter Sunday with snow on the ground. I wore a robe with weights sewn in the hem so it could not float up over my head. I waited in a dark hallway until I was called into the baptismal tank by the pastor. The water was heated. It sloshed over my face and hair. I waded out of the tank, blinking, right past the painted palms and into another dark hallway where there was a towel on a chair. I dried off in a washroom, changed back into my clothes, and returned to the church sanctuary looking about the same as I had a few minutes before.

The only member of the family at my baptism was my mother. No one hugged me. No one prayed over me before or after the event. Only one family wished me well afterward. My mother didn't stay, and I made my way to my aunt's house for the Easter meal alone and by bus. It was freezing out. No one mentioned the baptism at the family meal, and no one cared much about it except Mom.

A far cry, isn't it, from many baptisms you have witnessed and from many baptisms I have done, where there are all kinds of family and friends, hugs and prayers and clapping and worship songs, kind people with towels to help you when you are still half blind from the water, persons who want to celebrate with you and praise God with you? Mine was just an ordinary baptism—if there can be such a thing—and a pretty drab and uneventful one at that. Except on the inside. On the inside I was on fire.

I can't explain it. In that very ordinary and somewhat indifferent setting—no sunsets, no mountains, very little support, very little prayer and praise—I met God, and God met me. I felt like a living flame. I'd been ignited. The commitment I made in those few moments sparked an intimate experience with the risen Christ that glowed in me all day and all night and well into the week after. I felt I shone like diamonds, like silver, like sapphires. I felt as bright as light itself. Worship. Prayer. Bible reading. It all flowed like a fast, sleek river in my soul in the weeks and months that followed.

Of course, I can explain it. I had made a connection with Jesus, and I was permitted that day to feel it for all its worth. Baptism was a big deal, and I was allowed to know it for the big deal it was. Nothing much about my surroundings that day stirred my emotions or my spirit. It was all God. It had to be. And in my heart I celebrated and sang before the Lord.

THREE

He had disliked Jesus and Christianity all his life. Whenever he had a chance to mock it, he did so. Whenever he had a chance to drag its teachings through the dirt, he jumped at the opportunity. If he could hurt a Christian or tear apart one of their families or marriages, it was a high point in his week. As the years went by, his contempt and dislike grew into fury and hatred. It became an obsession with him to destroy whatever Christianity tried to build up. It was nothing less than a full-time occupation. He lived and breathed and slept hellfire.

One day he was blinded in a terrifying incident. It looked to him and the others who were with him at the time as if the blinding was irreversible. He was taken to a room in the house of a friend. Stunned by what had happened, he refused to eat or drink or leave the room. One day went by. And another. Then another. Finally, in his darkness, he began to pray.

A man found him at the house where he was holed up. The man asked if he could pray and then laid hands on him and said, "Brother Saul, the Lord—Jesus, who appeared to you on the road as you were coming here—has sent me so that you may see again and be filled with the Holy Spirit" (Acts 9:17). And the man who was blind saw again. Minutes later he was baptized. Then he ate for the first time in three days.

This man who had been blinded and then healed and baptized changed his name to Paul and became, of course, one of the great leaders and apostles of the Christian faith. He also became the most profound New Testament writer on what baptism means for the Christian.

In one of his earliest letters, Paul was already making inspired observations about the significance of baptism. In essence, he declared, "All Christ-followers are one. There should be no division between any of us. Christianity is not about whether you are a Greek or a Jew, whether you are free or a slave, whether you are a woman or a man. It's about Jesus, and we are all connected because of him": "All of you who were baptized into Christ have clothed yourselves with Christ" (Galatians 3:27).

When we make a fresh start to our day, we put on clean clothes. Paul is telling us that when we make a fresh start to our lives, we discard what we were before and put on Christ. This is what happens at baptism. The old garments that covered our soul are put aside. Jesus is now the garment that clothes and protects our spirit. And we see who our brothers and sisters are because they, too, are dressed in Christ. Baptism is the beginning of the Christian's new day, a day that never ends. We are not left soiled or naked. Jesus covers us.

That fact alone makes baptism much more than routine. So does the idea that all of us are one in Jesus. But as Paul thought and prayed and wrote over the years, God showed him other truths about baptism that he shared with the early churches. The one we probably know best is this: baptism imitates Christ's death and resurrection.

Don't you know that all of us who were baptized into Christ Jesus were baptized into his death? We were therefore buried with him through baptism into death in order that, just as Christ was raised from the dead through the glory of the Father, we too may live a new life.

Romans 6:3–4

You have observed baptisms and have heard these words, or something like them, used any number of times. As a pastor, I always use them. We bury a person in the water as we lower him or her, and this is a symbol of Christ's death and burial in the grave. As we lift the person out of the water, it symbolizes Christ's rising from the dead on Easter morning. His resurrection brings us new life as we rise from the deadness of our past and our sins into a fresh reality and an unstoppable future. It is a great wonder and a great mystery and a great truth that impacts every aspect of the rest of our lives.

Paul brings it up again when he writes the Christians in Colossae, reminding them that they have been buried with Christ "in baptism, in which you were also raised with him through your faith in the working of God, who raised him from the dead" (Colossians 2:12 TNIV). When he writes the Christians in Corinth, he tells them what he had told the Galatians: "We were all baptized by one Spirit so as to form one body—whether Jews or Gentiles, slave or free—and we were all given the one Spirit to drink" (1 Corinthians 12:13 TNIV).

Baptism is a way of totally identifying ourselves with Christ because we are buried as he was buried and we rise from the dead as he rose from the dead. It is an intimate and critical point of connection between our lives and his. But we are not only one with Jesus; we are also one with all those who believe in Jesus and are baptized in his name. In other words, there is not just a new me or you; there is a whole new people, a whole new race. Peter captures the sense of this when he writes, "You are a chosen people, a royal priesthood, a holy nation, God's special possession" (1 Peter 2:9 TNIV). Baptism not only changes persons; it changes the world.

So we see from the words of Paul and Peter and from the account of Jesus at the Jordan River how awesome baptism is. It is a symbol, but it is more than a symbol. It breathes a new breath of its own into the Christian life, and that breath is the breath of God. Some are afraid to give baptism much more than symbolic significance. They are worried that it will be treated as if it is some sort of magic add-on to the Christian life. Baptism is indeed powerful, but it is not powerful because it is magic; it is powerful because it comes from God the Father, connects a believer to God the Son at the crucial moment of his death and resurrection, and is vitalized by the Holy Spirit, who lives in those who believe. It does not save us. It is not some add-on to Christ's sacrifice on Calvary, but it brings home to us that work of Christ on the cross, and it's meant to make our salvation as plain as day to others and to ourselves.

What baptism signifies and represents and where it takes us are nothing less than divine acts of God. Of the water of the flood that floated the ark and saved Noah and his family, Peter writes, "This water symbolizes baptism that now saves you also

—not the removal of dirt from the body but the pledge of a good conscience toward God. It saves you by the resurrection of Jesus Christ" (1 Peter 3:21).

It is time we put aside the notion that baptism is a good and necessary but essentially formal and symbolic ritual that points to Christ's sacrifice on the cross yet brings no real power or vitality into the believer's life. Baptism is a God moment. That was so for Jesus, the divine Son of God, and it is so for us, who are saved by his death and resurrection and baptized into that death and resurrection in his holy and wonderful name.

FOUR

She put on her best dress. She had her hair done that morning. Favorite jewelry glittered at her throat and on her ears. She sat in her chair and let her friends place fresh towels over her chest and lap.

Helena was almost eighty. Although she had lots of energy she was also heavy, and her bones were frail. She had committed her life to Christ and wanted to be baptized, but she did not think she could handle an outdoor baptism or getting in and out of a baptismal tank. She also had a fear of being immersed in water, a fear of drowning.

So here we were in her small apartment. A basin with water in it sat at her feet. We prayed and sang, and I dipped a small bowl in the basin. As she declared before everyone in the room her faith in Christ, I poured the water from the bowl over her head. It ran down over her face and her dress and towels and hands and feet. And she beamed and sang and thanked God.

Baptism is a beautiful moment. At the Jordan River, the one God in three persons — the Father and the Son and the Holy Spirit — was present. At modern-day baptisms, there are also family and friends there, and usually lots of music and prayer support and a meal afterward. Even those who do not believe in Jesus show up at baptisms, not always because they have to, but often because they want to.

One summer day, we were doing a baptism in the creek that runs through our yard. This creek has its source high in the Rocky Mountains and runs green and clear through the foothills and plains after it leaves the great crags. Rainbow trout thrive in the fresh waters, and in our part of the world, where there are rainbow trout we usually find people fly-fishing who are hoping to catch a few of them. As our group came through the cottonwoods and assembled on the bank of the creek, I noticed several men fly-fishing nearby. I knew our gathering would likely disturb them. It would certainly disturb the trout, and I expected the men would reel in their lines and move further upstream or down.

They reeled in their lines all right, but they did not move on. Without speaking a word, they stood at a kind of attention with their tall rods glinting in the sunlight at their sides. Sunglasses and hats remained on; their waders were dark with the very water we were about to baptize in; their vests were bright with flies and hooks purple and green and red. They listened to everything we said, heard our songs, watched as each person was carried under the creek water by the hands of those who loved them and then carried back out again into the air and light. Only when we all came out of the water did they move on and begin to cast their lines into the green water once more. None of them came up to introduce themselves or tell me what church they belonged to, as many Christians might have done. They simply watched in silence and walked on in silence when the baptisms were done. Many see this point of connection between God and people by means of water as something holy and precious, even if they may not be people who believe in much that is holy and precious.

And that is why it is a tragedy that among many Christians the waters of baptism have divided churches instead of uniting them and blessing them. Infant baptism versus adult or believer's baptism, anointing with water or pouring versus full immersion, baptism that saves versus baptism that is a symbol of salvation — there is conflict and controversy about these things, and it is not just words that can become sharp and violent. In the past, thousands of Christians were killed by other Christians who did not like the way they practiced baptism. In the present, churches are shattered, relationships between Christians fractured, faith destroyed because baptism and love could not find common ground among the followers of Jesus. All this even though, as we have seen, Paul declared that everyone who is baptized in Christ is part of one body in Christ.

I prefer baptism by immersion, but I baptized Helena by pouring, and what happened to her was real. I have no doubt God met her in that small apartment. I prefer baptizing persons who are aware of what is going on and who are making their own choice to be baptized, but I have many Christian friends who were baptized as infants and who are part of Christian communities that baptize infants, and their hearts are full of love for Christ and the human race. I do not believe baptism saves anyone without them actually believing in Christ to begin with, and I do not believe that if an infant is not baptized and they die in their crib, they go to hell. But disagreement is not a time for hatred or cruelty; it is a time for prayer and listening and mercy. What good is my faith in Christ if it does not begin and end in love? What good is any church that does not evangelize and baptize in love? Does the world need more division and more hatred? Does it need more unkindness and viciousness, especially in the name of Jesus?

When I read the New Testament, especially the book of Acts, I see persons choosing to believe in Christ and then being baptized pretty much immediately — the mass baptisms on Pentecost when the Spirit fell (Acts 2:41), the Ethiopian eunuch (Acts 8:38), Lydia of Thyatira and her household (Acts 16:15), the Philippian jailer and his household (Acts 16:33), Cornelius the Roman and his friends and relatives (Acts 10:48).

Most churches don't carry out immediate baptism anymore. You believe in Christ, and then you wait and are taught doctrine — perhaps there is a catechism to learn — and if you are living a holy life, you are baptized months or years after you first believed. The people in Acts who were baptized only knew that Jesus had died to save them. They had no deep understanding at that point of the Incarnation or the Trinity or the distinctives of a Christian lifestyle. They just trusted Jesus to save them from their sins. And that was enough — not only for salvation but also for baptism.

So after my own study of the Scriptures, I have come to a place where I ask people to believe in Christ and be baptized — no waiting period, no gap. I do not ask them to lead a perfect life before they can be baptized, any more than a Christian church expects a person to lead a perfect life before they can believe in Jesus and be saved. The way I see it, baptism is joined at the hip with faith in Christ, and it naturally follows that if you have accepted Jesus as Savior and Lord, you should be baptized right away. In other words, baptism is meant to bless and help the young Christian right from the start. It is not meant to be a goal to aspire to or attain. It is not an achievement or a reward of righteous living, any more than salvation is. Baptism is the gift of God.

Now because of my beliefs does this mean I should start dividing churches, instigating quarrels, hurling vindictives against those who don't believe like I do, breaking off with other Christians who don't see things my way? Of course not. If churches want to ask new believers to wait a year before they are baptized, let them do so. If denominations want new believers to go through a catechism with a minister or priest, so be it. If some Christian communities want to see a new believer leading a holy life before they baptize them, then let the believer respect that. I am only saying I have found something I think is biblical and helpful and may be a blessing to those Christian communities that wish to take it up. It is certainly as valid as asking someone to take catechism classes or to clean up their lifestyle before they can enter the waters of baptism. It is something to think about, pray about, and talk about, but not fight about. We will never get rid of disagreements this side of heaven. Let's try not to get rid of love and mercy and grace either.

When I was a student in my early twenties at a Christian college, a group of young men and women decided that anyone who was not baptized went straight to hell when they died. Nothing could save you from that gruesome fate if you were not baptized. Water baptism was as critical to the salvation of the human soul as Christ's death on the cross. In fact, Christ's death on the cross could not help anyone who was not baptized.

·There was little love offered in the presentation of this doctrine. There was, however, plenty of anger and fury. I remember disagreeing with one of them, quite calmly too, as we drove into town one afternoon. Once we had parked, he got out, slammed his door and shook his fist at me, his face red and contorted. Baptism had divided believers once again instead of uniting us, as Paul taught. The beauty the fly fishermen saw that afternoon had become marred and grotesque.

Many of you have seen this sort of thing. The issue may not be baptism. It could be those who believe in the rapture of Christians arguing with those who believe Christians will go through the tribulation when it comes to the end-times. It could be a fight about a believer's free will versus God's sovereignty over all human affairs and decisions. It could be a clash between different factions in the church over the color of the new carpet, the length of the choir robes, or whether drums and electric guitars should be used in morning worship. We often do little to honor Christ's words that the world will know we're his disciples by the love we show toward one another.

It's not that people should never express their opinions, still less that believers ought never to stand up for what they believe is right, for what they see as the correct teachings of Christ and Christianity. It's how we go about doing it. So often we forget Paul's plea to speak the truth in love. A fine preacher I knew in my youth simply said, "If you can't go to someone you have an issue with and speak the truth in love, don't go." We might add some thoughts from Paul's immortal words about love in 1 Corinthians 13: If Christianity does not ultimately come down on the side of love, it is not Christianity.

FIVE

Lorine Jennifer was dying of AIDS contracted from a dirty needle. There was no reversing the process. She lost weight; her eye sockets became death hollows. She had no strength and no hope.

Her mother hovered over her in the hospital room, but her father never came. Her parents had been divorced for years, and he lived in another city. Still, she had been hospitalized for several weeks, more than enough time to book a flight.

"That man will never come," said her mother. "You left home and lived on the streets. He won't forgive you for that."

"But he'd already left us. He wasn't there. You were depressed. You told me to get out."

"I didn't mean it. That was the pills talking."

"He wasn't even there."

"The idea of his only child on the streets. He couldn't bear it. You disgraced him."

"But we used to go for those long walks in the park. Build fires together when we went camping. All the games."

"Those memories just make it harder for him. He won't come, Lorine Jennifer."

"Call him again."

"He won't come."

"Please call him again."

Her mother left to make the phone call, grumbling as she went out the door. Lorine Jennifer struggled to the washroom, her IV pole crashing along behind her. She fell to her knees, retching.

She was dying, and her father would not come.

That night after her mother had left, she asked the nurse to bring her more blankets. She was freezing, even though the temperature in the room was over eighty. When the nurse returned with the blankets, Lorine Jennifer began to talk, first about the weather — rain was splattering against her window — then about her mother, who drove the nursing staff crazy; and finally about her father, who would not come to her and hold her hand and sit by her bed. The nurse stayed longer than she should have. There were many patients who needed attention, and a number of medications to give out. But she felt she needed to stay. And when Lorine Jennifer began to wonder about life and death and heaven and hell and God, the nurse could not just get up and walk out the door — she was a Christian and often went to the hospital chapel on her breaks to think and pray in the quietness. So they talked about heaven and earth and God and love and Jesus. The nurse pulled a Bible from a drawer in the bedside table and showed Lorine Jennifer words the dying woman had never seen before. They hugged and prayed together before the nurse left.

In the dark Lorine Jennifer looked at the window that shone from the glow of a streetlight and thought of her father who would not come and God the Father who would, and of Jesus, who loved her without qualification. In the midst of the rain-drops she said, "I believe in you," and dropped off to sleep and never woke up again. The nurse found her at three in the morning and held her hand before calling another nurse to help her clean the body and wrap it gently in a white plastic shroud.

In this story, which is based on an actual event, a young woman commits herself to Christ and dies shortly afterward. This kind of thing is not rare. Deathbed conversions occur all the time. Sometimes the person is baptized right there in the hospital or at home. Under these circumstances, the baptism is usually done by anointing or sprinkling or pouring. But sometimes the person dies before they can be baptized—a soldier crying out to Christ for salvation as bullets tear his body apart, a woman praying to God as the airplane she is on crashes into the ground. What happens to them?

For many, perhaps most, this is a no-brainer. Persons are saved by faith in Christ. Period. Baptism is nice, and it gives us spiritual strength, but it is Christ's death on the cross that seals our souls for God. The thief on the cross was not baptized, was he? Yet Jesus said to him, "Today you will be with me in paradise" (Luke 23:43).

It's clear from Luke's account that baptism is not essential. My concern is that some people go to the opposite extreme on the basis of Luke 23:43 and say baptism is not necessary at all: "Do it, don't do it—it's not a big deal."

Yet as far as the first Christians were concerned, baptism was momentous. Notice how Peter defends water baptism for Cornelius and his friends: "Surely no one can stand in the way of their being baptized with water. They have received the Holy Spirit just as we have" (Acts 10:47 TNIV). As if no one would take issue with the fact that Romans could believe in Jesus or be filled with the Holy Spirit—but water baptism; wasn't that going too far?

For Ananias, who prayed over Paul so that he would see again, baptism was crucial and needed to be done as swiftly as possible: "And now what are you waiting for? Get up, be baptized and wash your sins away, calling on his name" (Acts 22:16). The Ethiopian eunuch felt the same way: "Look, here is water. What can stand in the way of my being baptized?" (Acts 8:36 TNIV). At midnight, just after the earthquake, the Philippian jailer took Paul and Silas and "washed their wounds; then immediately he and all his household were baptized" (Acts 16:33 TNIV).

There is a sense of urgency about baptism in the New Testament that many twenty-first-century churches seem to have lost. And not only a sense of urgency, but of importance. Baptism was not a take-it-or-leave-it proposition for the first Christians; it was critical and considered a great privilege. The special connection with God and his salvation and protection that it offered was considered too important to miss out on, too holy to hand out to just anyone, and far too significant to abstain from a minute longer than was necessary. For the first Christians, faith and baptism were one. Once you believed you had to be baptized in the name of Jesus. There was no argument. It was an enormous blessing from God that you needed to lay hold of right away.

Just before he left this earth, Jesus commanded that we make disciples of all nations, "marking them by baptism in the threefold name: Father, Son, and Holy Spirit" (Matthew 28:19 MSG). As in everything else, I believe the Lord knew what he was talking about when it came to water baptism. If he considered it important enough to emphasize in his parting message to his apostles and followers, it's safe to say we need to emphasize it in our speaking and praying and Christian living as well. Baptism matters.

The thief on the cross did not have a long life to live after he believed in Jesus. Nor do most people who have deathbed conversions. While it is true that none of us know the day and hour we will leave this earth, it's safe to say that most of the people who place their faith in Jesus Christ have months and years to live. They have a journey ahead of them and need all the help from God they can get. Water baptism is one of those great gifts from the Lord that give a believer faith, hope, and love. As the early Christians knew, it is something that must not be left out of the equation. Baptism cannot be window dressing or an afterthought. It is part and parcel of the salvation experience, of becoming a child of God. To neglect it is hazardous. To embrace it is new life and new strength.

SIX

There are rivers to cross, and then there are rivers to cross.

The bridge that crossed the water seemed flimsy at best and about to break in two at worst. A few boards, a few ropes, some twine—the kind of bridge that swings from side to side at the slightest breeze and drops your heart into your stomach.

The river itself was no bargain either—fast, cold, deep, fierce, roaring down out of the highest mountains in the world, the Himalayas.

I was trekking in Nepal in October. I wanted to reach Mount Everest's base camp or perhaps go even higher to the top of nearby Kala Pattar. From Pattar I could see everything—all of the south face of Everest and all of the high peaks surrounding it. Or so I'd been told. I wouldn't know for myself unless I crossed the bridge.

Countless Sherpas had crossed the bridge, as well as Buddhist monks, mountaineers from all over the world, trekkers like myself, men, women, children. From time to time there had been mishaps. Who knew what would happen today? I stood on one side and looked over to the other.

The big mountains were over that river. Some of the most stupendous landscapes on earth. Raw beauty, stunning vistas, a new world. All I had to do was cross.

This takes much longer to tell than it took me to decide. I hesitated for a moment or two, looked back at my companions, shrugged, snugged my pack tight on my back, and began the walk.

The bridge lurched. I staggered, braced myself, kept moving. Under my feet the river clawed its way through earth and stone as it had done for thousands of years. A river with an attitude.

If people were talking to me, I never heard them over the shout of the waters. Nor did I look down much at the green that bristled white over boulders and bank. I gripped the ropes strung on either side of me and carried on. It took only minutes. Soon I had my feet on the other shore and was laughing with my Nepalese guide and waiting for my friends to follow. Now I was in the land of the giants. And a few days later, I stood at the top of Kala Pattar at 18,500 feet and saw Everest's south face — all the peaks that surrounded it, clouds the color of light grazing the rock faces, and the earth slowly turning among the suns and stars of the universe. It was one of the great moments of my life. The river crossing brought me into a land and a life I had never experienced before, and it made a different person out of me.

The Jordan is a river of beginnings too, and not only because of baptism. It's also a river of beginnings for those who have crossed it. When Jacob returned to the Jordan after fleeing from his brother Esau, he was a new man — his name was Israel, and friendship had been restored between himself and his brother. For David too, when he returned after fleeing from his son Absalom, he was a chastened man, a different man, and a new king.

For the people of God, the story is even more significant. They had been liberated from Egypt. They had walked through the Red Sea. Doubting God, they had wandered through the desert for forty years. Now a new generation stood poised on the brink of entering the Promised Land — something neither their parents nor Moses would be able to do.

They knew that to go over the Jordan was to go to a place God had promised them for a homeland. They anticipated its beauty and fertility and spaciousness. But to experience all that God had prepared for them, they first had to cross.

The story is found in Joshua 3 and 4. The Jordan was at flood stage. But in a repeat of the Red Sea experience, as soon as the priests carrying the ark of the covenant touched the water, it stopped flowing and piled up at a town called Adam. The priests stood on dry ground in the middle of the Jordan, and all of Israel crossed over. The Bible says "the people hurried over" (Joshua 4:10). Twelve stones, representing the twelve tribes of Israel, were taken out of the Jordan in the place where the priests stood, and these stones were set up in the camp. "In the future," Joshua said, "when your children ask you, 'What do these stones mean?' tell them that the flow of the Jordan was cut off before the ark of the covenant of the LORD. When it crossed the Jordan, the waters of the Jordan were cut off. These stones are to be a memorial to the people of Israel forever" (verses 6 – 7). Once everyone was over and everything was completed, the priests carrying the ark left the Jordan and stood in the Promised Land with the others. Immediately the Jordan began to race between its banks at flood stage once again.

Like Jesus after his new beginning at the baptism in the Jordan, Israel would be tested in the days and weeks to come. Jesus emerged from his testing stronger, "in the power of the Spirit" (Luke 4:14), and began the life he had come to earth to live. Israel emerged a nation and, despite many ups and downs, gave the world the Messiah, "a light for revelation to the Gentiles," as Simeon put it, holding the infant Jesus in his arms, "and for glory to your people Israel" (Luke 2:32).

We have our baptisms and start anew; we also cross our rivers and start anew. There are all kinds of rivers God calls us to cross, all kinds of Jordans. He asks us to take the steps of faith that will usher us into a new relationship, a new career, a new ministry, a new country. Do we trust him? Or do we waste time wandering in the desert? He asks us to cross over and do something completely different, to leave our old lives behind and strike out in a new direction with his blessing, to start from scratch, to do things for him we've never done before—and he guarantees he will be with us. Do we trust him? Everything has fallen apart—we're afraid, not sure where to go and what to do—and the Lord invites us to cross the Jordan of disappointment into a new land, a new opportunity, a new experience of his love and grace. Do we believe him? The Jordans we cross under the hand of God determine what sort of person and what sort of Christian we are going to be.

Although that bridge and river were perhaps my greatest test, I crossed many other bridges and rivers afterward. And in one of them, I had to do something I swore I would not do, namely, clean my body and my hair.

We had been trekking for days and weeks. I did not want to get a skin rash or an infection, especially one that might disable me before I reached Everest Base Camp or the peak of Kala Pattar. It's not that I was adverse to keeping clean. I used a wet cloth every day to clean myself up. But spot-cleaning of your body with a wet rag doesn't always do the trick. What I didn't want to do I eventually did—bathe myself in one of the icy rivers.

So I slipped out of sight one morning, took off my clothes, and slipped into the fast water of one of the rivers. It was bone-crunching cold, as I knew it would be. Quickly I used sand and grit to scour my body and hair. I froze up within seconds. When I plunged my head under the current, my brain went numb.

Did I tell you I was one-handed during this body-cleansing operation? The other hand desperately gripped a thick tree branch so I wouldn't be swept down thousands upon thousands of feet to Kathmandu. During the few minutes I washed my skin and abrasions and sores, the one consolation was the fact the water was incredibly pure, leaping from the snows and glaciers at the very top of the world, scarcely touched by oxygen, let alone anything else. I suppose I could have shelled out dozens of rupees for heated water and some sort of tub of wood or metal, but in the end being washed clean by the unspoiled Himalayan waters was best. Once I toweled myself off, brushed my hair, and put on clean clothes, I felt like a new man.

Later that day, my feet feeling invigorated and my blisters closing up and healing, I had hiked a good distance and began to see some of the peaks for which the region is famous. I caught my first glimpse of Everest in the distance—the locals call it

Sagarmatha or Big Boy—and was properly awed as I saw its head emerge grandly from the afternoon cloud and mist. I saw another peak that definitely had a presence, towering over us as we walked, and towering over clouds and lesser peaks as well.

"Which one is that?" I asked my Sherpa guide.

"Ama Dablam," he told me. "The Hand of God."

You will remember that Jesus provoked a great deal of anger in his hometown of Nazareth by pointing out that God did not show favoritism to Israel. In fact, people who had been his neighbors for close to thirty years tried to push him off a cliff and murder him. One of the examples he cited that inflamed them was that of Naaman, who was the commander of the army of the king of Aram: "There were many in Israel with leprosy in the time of Elisha the prophet, yet not one of them was cleansed—only Naaman the Syrian" (Luke 4:27).

The story of Naaman's cleansing is found in 2 Kings. He came to Israel for help, and Elisha told him to dip in the Jordan River seven times. Naaman, a bit of a nationalist himself (like the people of Nazareth), at first refused: "I thought that he would surely come out to me and stand and call on the name of the LORD his God, wave his hand over the spot and cure me of my leprosy. Are not Abana and Pharpar, the rivers of Damascus, better than any of the waters of Israel? Couldn't I wash in them and be cleansed?" (2 Kings 5:11–12). But his servants convinced him to do what Elisha said. So he went in and out of the Jordan seven times, perhaps with a bit of the same reluctant spirit that I dipped myself in that brisk river of Nepal, "and his flesh was restored and became clean like that of a young boy" (verse 14).

This healing in the Jordan River changed Naaman's life, not surprisingly, considering how deadly a disease leprosy is. It brought him to a faith in God. "Now I know," Naaman declared to Elisha, "that there is no God in all the world except in Israel" (2 Kings 5:15). He then asked God's forgiveness for having to bow while he assisted the king of Aram to bow in the temple of Rimmon. Elisha told Naaman, "Go in peace" (verse 19).

Once again, as in baptisms and in life crossings, the Jordan River comes to stand for new beginnings—in this case, healings and, in a way, unexpected healings that bring a person to a new or renewed faith. I say unexpected because Naaman had his own idea of how he wanted to be healed, and he clung to it. But it wasn't God's way, and he almost missed out on the healing because of it. We also can come to God for help and healing with a fixed notion of how it must be done—through a certain doctor at a certain hospital, at a certain prayer meeting at a certain church, at a certain time of day alone in our room. "What? God wants to use that doctor? I hate that doctor!" "What? A prayer meeting at that church with that pastor? I don't like that church, and I don't like that pastor!" "What? Not alone in my room? In public? In front of all those people? No way!" And because we cannot conceive—or don't want to conceive—of God working in a way different from ours, we lose out on his blessing, at least for a time, until we can rearrange our thinking and our priorities to line up with his.

When I was young, I once called on God to help me financially so that I could be part of an overseas mission trip. I certainly felt led to go, and I fasted and prayed for a week that the money I needed would come in. Some money, of course, did come in through the job I had, but I needed more. I thought God would work through my church, but the church wasn't enthusiastic about my sense of mission and didn't support me. I thought the money would show up once I had completed my week of fasting, but nothing came in the mail or was dropped off at the door. In fact, nothing happened in the way I'd envisioned it, and the deadline drew near.

Part of preparing for this mission trip required visits to the public health nurse on a regular basis and getting a series of immunizations against various diseases. At the beginning of my time of prayer and waiting, getting these shots was easy to do because I was full of faith and confidence. After weeks and months had gone by, I wasn't so enthusiastic about getting my arm punctured again and again. But I carried on nonetheless. I suppose, at the end of it all—because I was feeling pretty discouraged—it was the little bit of faith I could still muster that God had called me to a summer mission. The way this story goes, there's no way I can claim credit for anything except perhaps a dogged insistence that somehow God was in this and would show up and restore my hope. The very last day of the very last needle poke, as I sat on a bench outside the clinic waiting for a bus, a Christian friend who had accompanied me handed me a white unmarked envelope containing all the necessary finances. To this day she will not tell me who felt led to do this.

I had my own timetable and my own plan; God had his. I'm glad I didn't give up. I'm glad I kept dipping in the Jordan, as I'd been told to do—even if, like Naaman, I did so somewhat reluctantly, even resentfully. When God acted in his way and in his time, it healed my soul and restored my faith — in fact, it increased my faith. That overseas mission experience affected me for life.

Thank God for all the Jordan Rivers in our lives. Let's pray we have the faith to see them for the opportunities that they are — and not turn away from the hand of God out of our assumption that the way in which God would choose to give us new life and a new beginning could not possibly look like what, in fact, is the very sign of his presence.

SEVEN

The man used his brush swiftly. He made the land, the trees, the people, the sky. Then he got down to business: clouds breaking, a dove descending, Jesus, then finally the river itself. The banks of the river he made the color of light. Jesus too, and the dove and the clouds. But the river he made black. As death.

Two weeks after Christmas each year, our Orthodox friends celebrate the baptism of Jesus in the Jordan River at the Feast of Theophany. A theophany is the appearance or manifestation of God to human eyes, and in the case of Christ's baptism we see the Trinity (Father, Son, Holy Spirit)—one God. The painter of the icon made the Jordan dark because it symbolizes death. When new believers are baptized, they are buried with Christ. In a way, the first part of a believer's baptism is a personal experience of Good Friday—Christ's crucifixion and death. On the other hand, baptism is also an Easter experience because it is about Christ's resurrection as well. We are raised up out of the water to new life in Christ.

So perhaps our artist could make a triptych, three panels hinged together with three different paintings on them—one of the Jordan before Jesus enters the water, looking like a normal river; one of the Jordan with Jesus being baptized in it, the river dark to signify his death and burial; the final a painting of the

Jordan as Jesus emerges from the water, the dove on his shoulder, the sky opened up with the Father's voice—this time the river is gold to symbolize Christ's victory over death and therefore the believer's victory also. For on the eve of the Feast of Theophany the priest prays, "Thou hast descended into the waters and hast given light to all things, that they may glorify Thee, O Savior, the Enlightenment of our souls."

The Jordan is a God symbol and a Christ symbol, as potent in its own way as the cross or the manger or the empty tomb. The Jordan is also a symbol of new life from baptism, of healing, and also of crossing over to a new land and a new commitment to God. In baptism, the idea is one of passing from death to life through the death and resurrection of Jesus. A healing or cleansing is like coming back to life, and the life you have come back to live in God is much different from the one you left. A crossing over is moving from what was to what will be, from the past to the future, with that future securely in the hands of God.

So the Jordan is really a river of renewal and a river of life—and God life at that. No wonder Africans and African-Americans in the American South saw the Jordan as a holy symbol of heaven and eternity when they sang "Roll, Jordan, Roll":

Roll, Jordan, roll
Roll, Jordan, roll
I want to go to heaven when I die
To hear old Jordan roll

O brother you ought to've been there, Yes my Lord
A-sittin' up in the kingdom

To hear old Jordan roll
Sing it over

O sinner you ought to've been there
A-sittin' up in the kingdom
To hear old Jordan roll

Roll, Jordan, roll
Roll, Jordan, roll
I want go to heaven when I die
To hear old Jordan roll

PART FIVE

THE SEA OF GALILEE

The WATERS *of* GOD *with* US

*When Jesus had again crossed over by boat
to the other side of the lake, a large crowd
gathered around him while he was by the lake.*
Mark 5:21

ONE

There are certain sounds that stir my blood and place me instantly at one with the wilderness of our created earth — the moan of the wolf, the cry of the coyote, the trumpet of the elk, and the wail of the loon.

It was the loon that got me out of the cabin and down to the lake. Mist rose from the water in gray streamers. The sun was not yet up, but the clearness of the sky and the bright stab of the last stars promised a hot day. I untied a red canoe and began to paddle.

Depending on which book you look at, I grew up by a body of freshwater that is the twelfth or thirteenth largest in the world. It was more like an inland sea than a lake. Summer and winter storms threw up ocean-sized waves that hammered the land like breakers on saltwater rocks. Sailboats drifted over its broad and deep surface. There were gulls and pelicans and ospreys. And a vastness that blurred the edge of water and sky.

My parents used to take us to a lake every summer and rent a cabin. We swam, had picnics on the beach, and walked in the forest. On stormy days we got to hurl ourselves into tall gray waves that rocked our bodies and brains. Afterward, we could sit in the cabin in a hoodie and play board games and card games or read books. Nowadays, you'd watch TV or DVDs or play computer games or listen to your iPod. I like DVDs and CDs and surfing the net, but if I were at that cabin again, I'd keep it the way it was.

A lake is something very special, different from the river or the sea. It has places near its shores that remind you of the Shenandoah or the Red where they wind and bend under painted trees. It has other places that surge and roll and toss up whitecaps like the Atlantic or the Pacific. Yet its charm is that it can be more idyllic than both. How many sunsets and sunrises of great peace do I remember near some lake's still waters, near its islands and boulders and firs? How many times have I sat by a campfire's smoke and flame and listened to people tell stories or talk about God or laugh at laughter, while behind me the lake lapped the land like a cat laps milk? How often have I run and leaped and fought my friends in waters that held no bite of salt or curse of shark or sting of jellyfish? A lake is one of the greatest gifts of a great God.

Henry David Thoreau might have agreed with me. For him, a lake was "the landscape's most beautiful and expressive feature. It is earth's eye; looking into which the beholder measures the depth of his own nature." William Wordsworth thought along the same lines, declaring that "a lake carries you into recesses of feeling otherwise impenetrable."

So I took the canoe, as a boy who has summered on lakes is taught to do. I had not seen a loon in months. The cries and wails intensified and rang from shore to shore as I approached. Their language pulled me into a head space and heart space where seeing God was as easy as breathing and faith as natural as my steady strokes through the water—water like cream, paddle swirls like froth, the air and mist and lake one long tunnel opening to light and greenness and black-and-white heads popping in and out of the water.

What made this morning a memory that did not get lost in that vast soup of all my pleasant memories was how close the loons let me get to them. I thought they would just dive and then bob up a hundred feet from the threatening scarlet of my sharp-prowed vessel. Instead they stayed up and laughed by my side in their strange red-eyed way, and I laughed with them. Peeling back the dawn to a white August sun, God joined us that daybreak and laughed heartily, just as he had laughed by another lake's shores so many years before.·

TWO

The man smiled and laughed and nodded and stepped toward the boat with the yellow hull, swinging aboard like someone accustomed to vessels and hulls and rigging.* The crowd laughed and applauded. Many of them were already standing in the lake. Where else was he supposed to go so everyone could catch a glimpse of him? Three or four of the fishermen and one of their wives pushed the boat out from the beach and then held one of its thick ropes so it would not drift too far.

It was hot. Jesus peeled off his robe and pushed up the sleeves of the tunic he wore underneath. There was some water in the bottom of the boat, and he splashed his face with it and ran his wet hands through his hair. A bird landed on the mast and cocked its head at him. A little girl pointed. Jesus looked and grinned and said to the girl, "Listen, how would you like to hear a story that has birds in it?"

She ducked her head, suddenly shy, and stirred some stones with her bare toe. "*Kin*," she said in Aramaic. "Yes, all right."

"Well," Jesus began, "there was a farmer, a good man, and he wanted to plant some wheat so he could make bread. He scattered the seed on the ground, you know, like this"— flinging

---

* The stories in this chapter are based on the biblical accounts in Mark 4–6 and the parallel passages in Matthew 8–9 and 13–14; Luke 8–9 and 13; and John 6.

out his hand, clenching and unclenching his fist — "but what do you think happened? Our bird friend here and his whole family were very hungry. They saw the man throwing the seed out on the ground and said to one another, "Why let that seed go to waste? So down they swooped and ate the seeds they could most easily get at — the ones that fell on the road."

He had plenty of stories to tell that day — ones about lamps on tables, about people who plant fields and forget they planted them, fields that grow tall and get ripe behind their backs. There were stories about weeds and good plants growing together, about hidden treasures and once-in-a-lifetime pearls. There was one about a tiny mustard seed, like a tiny girl, shooting up so big and strong that the tiny girl's bird friends could perch on its thickest branches. This is what God's world is like, he kept saying, like the best treasure, the best pearl, the seeds that start small and then become so much more — a quiet start and then, whoosh, God-life is everywhere! He always had a story. And he always had someone to listen.

After The Sermon in the Boat, his closest friends asked him to explain in detail what each story meant. Jesus did that. Then he wanted to take the boat to the other side of the lake — the vessel with the yellow hull actually belonged to one of his friends. As they got in and set sail, other boats crowded around them with their red and green and blue hulls and sailed alongside, calling and waving. Jesus stood and waved for a bit, especially to the little girl, then helped get the lines tight. But he was tired from all his talking and needed a nap.

He fell into one of those sleeps in which you'd have to set

fire to a person in order to wake them. The wind suddenly picked up, and a storm blew in. Many of the boats turned back. Waves cracked into their hull and started breaking over the boat, and the fishermen friends of Jesus grew frightened. They hauled down the sail, but it didn't make much of a difference. The boat pitched back and forth, and they were ankle-deep in water. Jesus slept on. They crowded around him, panicked, and shook him: "We're going to die!"

Jesus blinked and woke up, looked at them, looked at the storm, got to his feet and said to the squall, "Enough! Calm down!" And the storm stopped. This frightened his friends even more. "Who is this?" But Jesus, perhaps a bit annoyed at being woken up out of a sound sleep, said to them: "After all we've been through and all you've seen—where's your faith?" Then they landed the boat on the far shore of the lake—and there they met Legion.

The friends were frightened afresh as a wild man flew out of the graveyard at them, streaming blood and shrieking with the strength of a thousand voices. Jesus stood his ground. It was not the man; it was what was in the man that was wrong.

"Wicked spirit! Get out of him! Now!" snapped Jesus.

"Jesus! Son of the Most High God! Leave me alone! Don't hurt me!" roared the man, crashing to his knees.

"What is your name?" demanded Jesus.

"Legion. For we are many. Don't hurt us. Don't send us far away. Let us go into those swine feeding over there."

"Go!"

The swine went wild and rushed down a cliff and into the

lake and drowned. There were two thousand of them. The swineherds ran and told the people in the town nearby, and they rushed out to see what was going on. They found the madman clothed and calm and dead animals floating in the water. If the friends of Jesus were a bit overwhelmed by what they had just seen happen, the townspeople felt even more alarmed. "Please, whoever you are," they pleaded with Jesus, "get out of here and leave us alone."

So Jesus got back into the boat. The madman, who was now the good man, sound in mind and body, tried to get into the boat with him. Jesus shook his head. "It's time your family had you back within their four walls again; they've been without you long enough. Go to them. Tell them what God has done for you. Let them see for themselves how much he loves you." Jesus gripped his shoulder and smiled. The friends pushed the boat into the water and hoisted the sail, and Jesus was gone.

They reached the shore they had left, and people were there, desperate for his love and healing—Jairus, whose daughter was dying, as well as a woman who had been hemorrhaging for twelve years. The woman touched the hem of his robe, and her bleeding stopped. The little girl died, but Jesus said to her father, "Don't be afraid; just believe," went to the girl's room, held her hand, spoke the words, *"Talitha koum!"* and the girl lived again. Everyone was astounded. Jesus simply said, "Listen, you need to give her something to eat."

There were many more healings and many more stories to tell up and down the shore of the lake. After days and weeks of intense activity, Jesus shook his head and looked at his friends.

"This is a bit much, isn't it? You can't even sit down and get a bite to eat without another person coming along and wanting help. You need a break. Let's get in the boat and find a place where you can get some rest."

They pushed the boat out into the lake and went a short distance to a quiet shore where there were only birds and breezes. For a few moments in the boat, they had peace and quiet. But people followed them and arrived at the destination ahead of them. Jesus felt sorry for them. They were in so much need, not just for physical healing, but for something to believe in, to give their lives purpose. So he talked to them all, and when it got late, he told his friends to feed them.

Just like that! Thousands of people! It couldn't be done!

But Jesus took what little there was—five loaves of bread and two fish—blessed the food, and everyone was fed. The mustard seed had grown into a tree. Then he sent the people home, told his friends to sail on ahead of him into Bethsaida, and walked alone into the hills so he could pray without disruption.

His friends didn't make much headway. A wind came up against them, and they had to drop the sail and ply the oars. It was tough work. They were at it for hours but made very little progress. So Jesus came to them early in the morning, after they'd been at the oars most of the night—walking right to them on the water.

Of course they didn't know it was him. The night was dark, they were tired, and they'd never seen anyone walk on top of a lake before. Once more, fear gripped them: "It's a ghost!" But Jesus spoke up immediately, "Don't be afraid! It is I!"

They weren't sure. Peter called, "If it really is you, Lord, tell me to join you on the water."

"Come on," Jesus said.

So Peter stepped out of the boat onto the lake. The water held firm. He splashed toward Jesus—it was like walking through a long puddle that had hard ground underneath. It was strange and exhilarating at the same time. "This can't be happening," thought Peter. "I've got to be dreaming." But the water was real enough. And the wind, which threw waves up against his body. *My God, I'm going to die!* Peter began to sink like a stone. "Jesus," he cried out in terror, "save me!"

Jesus didn't waste any time. He grabbed Peter and kept him above water. "Peter," he said, "what happened to your faith? Why did you doubt?"

They both got into the boat. Immediately the wind dropped, and it was calm. Again. The friends were stunned. "You're the Son of God!" they said to Jesus. In no time at all, they touched land at Gennesaret. They looked at Jesus and at one another. It was dawn.

But they had no time to absorb what they had just seen or try to figure out what it meant. People recognized Jesus and began bringing their sick to him. Soon there were crowds around them again—everywhere they went along the shores of the lake.

THREE

Locals also called the Sea of Galilee the Sea of Tiberias (John 6:1) and the Lake of Gennesaret (Luke 5:1). I suppose it was called a sea because of its size and its weather — at thirteen miles long it is the largest lake in Israel, subject to winds and storms that some days seem to rival the open waters of the Mediterranean.

Its lifeblood is the Jordan River. The Jordan comes down out of the mountains, feeds it, then flows south all the way to the Dead Sea, which is also a lake. In fact, the two lakes that are lowest in elevation in the entire world are the Dead Sea and the Sea of Galilee, forever linked by the river that provided the water for the baptism of Jesus.

Many famous events in the life of Jesus take place on or near the Sea of Galilee — the calming of the storm, the feeding of the five thousand, the Garasene demon-possessed man, the walking on water, the "*Talitha koum*" that raised Jairus's daughter from the dead, the parable of the sower and the seed. Yet when we put the lake stories all together, as I did in the previous chapter, what strikes me is how much human fear there is — fear that is conquered not through faith in ourselves but through faith in Jesus.

There is fear of nature. The storm on the lake had the disciples terrified that they were going to die, and the wind on the lake had Peter frightened that he was going to drown. Jesus — and this often happens — is bewildered by their inability to trust that things will turn out all right when he is around: "Why are you so afraid? Do you still have no faith?" (Mark 4:40). Throughout his life on earth, he was always exasperated that people just didn't get it: "I and the Father are one" (John 10:30).

There is fear of evil and also of those who challenge evil. The man who was possessed was so violent no one could pass near him (Matthew 8:28). Yet when Jesus dealt with the man and freed him of his evil spirits, the people who lived there and knew the man wanted Jesus gone. His holy power was more frightening to them than the unholy power they were accustomed to seeing from the madman (Mark 5:16–17).

There is fear of death. When Jairus's daughter dies, men come from his house and tell Jairus it's over. Whatever Jesus might have been able to do can't be done now. Jesus challenges Jairus not to be overcome by his fear of the power of death because the power of Jesus is greater: "Don't be afraid; just believe" (Mark 5:36).

There is fear of inadequacy, inability, and impossibility. The disciples know they can't feed the crowd Jesus asked them to feed. It would take almost a year's wages, and no one had that kind of money. But even if they did, they were out in the wilderness. There were no stores or bakeries or butchers nearby. Sure, they had a couple of fish and maybe five loaves of bread — realistically, what could a person do with that to feed thousands? Nothing could be done. Why was Jesus stressing them out by telling them to feed everyone? Jesus wanted them to learn that when he was around and asked them to do something, what little they could do or give was enough for the task at hand: "If you have faith as small as a mustard seed, you can say to this mountain, 'Move from here to there,' and it will move. Nothing will be impossible for you" (Matthew 17:20).

There is fear of the supernatural and the occult. The disciples are certain a ghost is coming after them across the water. Jesus has to reassure them quickly that they are not being haunted: "Take courage! It is I. Don't be afraid" (Mark 6:50).

There is fear of Jesus. We see this in the reaction of the people to the deliverance of the demon-possessed man and the death of the herd of swine, but we also find that the disciples often don't know what to make of Jesus either. After the quieting of the storm, "they were terrified and asked each other, 'Who is this? Even the wind and the waves obey him!'" (Mark 4:41). This is not the kind of biblical fear of God that produces awe and reverence and respect; this is more like the fright they experienced when they thought they saw a ghost. The more time they spent with Jesus, the more this kind of fear went away. Astounded by his act of walking on the water, they worshiped him (Matthew 14:33). Yet when he rose from the dead years later, they thought he was a spirit once again, just as they had when he walked on the lake: "They were startled and frightened, thinking they saw a ghost" (Luke 24:37).

Usually these stories are taught in our churches by way of a negative example—of declaring what not to do when God asks you to have faith. How many times have you heard it said, "Peter took his eyes off Jesus, and that's when he started to sink"? In other words, don't you be foolish like Peter, or you'll sink too.

How many times have you heard messages belittling the disciples for not trusting Jesus to calm the storm, not trusting Jesus to take care of the five thousand? And to go beyond the lake stories, how many times have you heard the disciples mocked because they did not understand the crucifixion and did not believe in the resurrection, even though Jesus had told them about these things on several different occasions?

The same mockery often extends to the lack of faith on the part of Israel, both before they entered the Promised Land and after. Why do they keep making such a mess of things? Why can't they just trust God? Why don't they stick to his commands and have more faith?

Would we have done any better than the disciples or the children of Israel?

Think about the times people like you and me have let God down. Think about the times we didn't obey. Think about the times we didn't think he could quell a storm in our lives. Think about the times he asked us to walk on that water with him, and we couldn't do it.

What about the times he gave us five loaves and two fish, and we said, "No way! That's nowhere near enough to work with"? Or the times he asked us to approach the death of a loved one without fear and in total trust, and we gave in to fear and grief and didn't trust him at all? What about those seasons of our lives when we hardly had any love for Jesus but feared him instead, the way a person fears supernatural forces or a ghost?

Yet here is the great thing about the lake stories. I don't believe they are meant to be used in this way. I don't believe they are included in Scripture to make us feel bad about the disciples or about ourselves. I don't think they've been preserved for all of human history to slap us down; I think they're in the Bible to pull us up.

Take a look at the storm. Yes, the disciples panicked. Yes, Jesus gave them a bit of a hard time for not having enough faith. Yet he stopped the storm. And really, this was for their benefit. According to him, no one was in any danger. It was for their sake he calmed the squall, not his. I don't know about you, but I'm used to persons who are in charge under similar difficult circumstances and who want to use the fear experience to teach valuable life lessons—so they don't stop the incident from happening. They make you and everyone else go through it to make sure you will be stronger for the next time that something terrifying occurs. Jesus didn't think that way. He had compassion.

Take a look at the feeding of the five thousand. No, the disciples didn't have faith that anything could be done. Jesus doesn't say, "OK, fine. You still don't believe in me, so stand off to the side and let me do it for myself." He gets them involved. They come up with the five loaves and two fish, hand out the food to the crowd, and gather up the leftovers when the meal is done. By keeping them in the experience instead of excluding them for their lack of faith, he makes sure they see for themselves the miracle that occurs. It helps them grow and change. It helps them have faith they didn't have before.

Take a look at Peter walking on water. He actually gets out

of the boat and starts walking. He loses his nerve after a few moments, but he made the first effort. Jesus was disappointed that Peter lost focus. But he didn't say, "Well, you need to learn a lesson about this. There's no time like now. Sink or swim, Peter"—and then leave him for a few minutes to have something of a drowning experience so he'd remember to have more faith next time. Jesus reached out and rescued him and accompanied Peter back into the boat.

All the lake stories—and a whole lot more—are like that. Jesus treats the madman with compassion before and after his deliverance. When people are afraid of his powers and want him gone, he gets into the boat and leaves and doesn't call down fire on their village. When the disciples think he's a ghost, he doesn't lecture them about superstition and faith; he takes away their fear by saying, "Take courage! It is I. Don't be afraid" (Mark 6:50). When pain and grief stab Jairus's soul after being told of his daughter's death, Jesus immediately knows and cares about what Jairus is going through: "Don't be afraid; just believe" (Mark 5:36). When the disciples are terrified of his powers once they see him stop the storm, he does not dress them down or leave them to stew in their fear or decide he shouldn't let them see his powers again for a long time. Instead, in quick succession, he exposes them to a confrontation with evil spirits, the healing of a woman who was hemorrhaging, and the raising back to life of a dead twelve-year-old girl. The disciples—not just the three who'd seen it firsthand—and family, friends, neighbors, relatives, and mourners "were completely astonished" (Mark 5:42).

Jesus' grace and love are so obvious in the lake stories that it should be enough for us to realize that when Jesus sets the bar and we don't make it over, he will not hate and despise us and leave us to rot because we don't have enough faith. Others might—and even other Christians might abandon us. Jesus will have compassion on us and help us get to our feet and try again. And again. He never gave up on his disciples, and eventually they changed the entire world. He will never give up on us either.

FOUR

It was just a hike up a mountain. We looked forward to it, and we weren't concerned about hazards we might run into on the way. After all, we had been up mountains in Canada and the United States. What could a mountain in Scotland do to us?

It was The Ben, mind you — Ben Nevis, the highest mountain in the British Isles — so we made sure we had plenty of gear and tons of food and water. We intended to stop at a lake or loch halfway up for the overnight and then get to the summit the next morning and come down. It was a good plan, we thought.

We headed up from the youth hostel early in the morning. At first there was a great deal of mist. Later it burned off and we had a nice blue June Scottish sky over our heads for the rest of the day. I think what surprised my friend and me was how precipitous the route was in some places — the skinny path barely wide enough for a couple of boots. But we were at the loch in short order and pitched our sturdy tent, cooked some soup over a kerosene stove, and wandered the moor for several hours until the stars winked into sight.

That night a storm blew in — a not uncommon occurrence for The Ben, we found out later, but certainly not expected by us. The wind grew so ferocious we got out of our tent and laid the poles flat so they wouldn't be bent out of shape and rendered useless for any future expeditions. For a long time, the tent kept the moisture out, but by daybreak water began to work its way in from seams in the corners, even though they'd been taped and waterproofed.

There wasn't much we could do outside of our pancaked tent. Gray clouds streaked over the moor like bony fingers, and I felt we would see the witches from *Macbeth* at any moment. It was freezing outside but warm in our sleeping bags. We munched on our cold rations, especially fortified chocolate bars. We kept waiting for the weather to break, but it never did.

Eventually our bags began to sop up the water that snuck in. This made the wet parts of our bags useless for heat retention. The goose feathers were all matted together and lost their loft. There were no down bags coated with waterproofing in those days, or if there were, we couldn't afford them. We didn't have covers for our bags either—an item we would rarely have used back home unless we lived in the Pacific Northwest near Seattle or Vancouver. So we began to grow colder and colder. By evening I began to worry about another stormy night and the possibility of hypothermia. Still, parts of our bags were dry, so we stayed in them.

We spoke to each other now and then. There wasn't much to talk about. I read Job by what light there was and then used my flashlight for awhile. I prayed for the storm to cease, tossing and turning during the night from anxiety and cold chills. I kept seeing a sign I'd glanced at in the hostel reporting that 256 people — or something like that — had died on ascents of Ben Nevis since the 1950s, usually due to being caught out in the frequent and bitter weather systems that assaulted the mountain. I hadn't paid much attention to the sign. Now I honestly wondered if this was the way it was going to end and whether some painter would grumble about having to change his 6 into an 8 (not too hard, I thought).

The pewter morning promised no relief. Visibility was so poor I couldn't see more than an arm's length in front of me. How could we make a descent in these conditions? A slip would be easy, a fall even easier. So should we stay in the flattened tent and go slowly or take a risk in the fog and go quickly? I prayed some more and actually finished all 42 chapters of Job.

Then, unbelievably, as I looked out of the tent at the woolly gray moor and sky, I saw a ragged patch of blue sailing toward us from the sea. It was moving along at a pretty good clip, caught up in the storm system, and we both reckoned it would be over our heads in about ten minutes. It gave us a shot of hope, and we acted. We rolled up the tent and our soggy down bags and helped each other get the packs onto our backs in the driving rain and sleet. When the blue sky hit, we headed briskly down the mountain.

We knew the break in the storm would not last long, and we were right. But it lasted long enough for us to get past the trickiest parts on the trail, and we could see everything clearly as if we were marching through a high-resolution photograph. Near the bottom, the Scottish pipes opened, and it began to pour again, but by then we had the hostel in sight. I remember a young American gasping as I pulled off one of my boots at the door and emptied it of water. The brown stream kept coming and coming. It seemed like there were quarts of it.

We were alive, and I thanked God for calming the storm during that short interval. It seems to me to have been too brief a period of time to have been the storm's eye, and the wind didn't completely drop either. I think of it as a storm bubble of clear sky and dry air that God made sure came winging our way. I can say the experience both increased my faith and increased my caution. I have been back to Scotland since that day, but never back to The Ben. Hopefully I will get there again and make it safely to the summit next time around, with God still at my side.

FIVE

All of us have stories about God asking us to start something big with meager resources — our "five loaves and two fish" stories. I think most of us also have stories about God asking us to step out of our safe boats and walk in faith the kind of walk we have never undertaken before. Here is one of those stories.

I didn't see it coming — but neither did the disciples who were bent over their oars and plowing into the wind. I was rowing away in my own fashion at my college studies — at Hebrew and Greek and scads of other subjects — when I went to morning chapel and listened to a guest speaker from Northern Ireland. His words astonished me. Former Loyalist and IRA gunmen coming to faith in the real Jesus at the Maze Prison nine miles outside of Belfast. Praying together. Reading the Bible together. Wasn't this the kind of reconciliation and transformation Jesus gave his life to bring to the world? When he said he was looking for volunteers to come to Belfast that summer and work with his organization and various churches to bring Christ's love to Ireland, I put a leg over the side of my cozy North American college boat.

I was ready to walk the walk. But later, when I delved into what they wanted me to do in Northern Ireland, I balked — open-air public speaking, public speaking in churches, open-air drama and music, children and youth work, door-to-door ministry—no way did I want to do public speaking outdoors at market days or rallies, and no way did I want to go door-to-door with leaflets in my hand. The wind was picking up, and the waves were getting higher. I lost my nerve and quickly clambered back into the boat. I hardly got my feet wet.

God let it go. Or at least he appeared to. I went on with my studies and forgot about Ireland. Other people I knew were making plans to head over during the summer and praying about the mission and about funding. Good for them. I finished the term at Christmas, took my exams, and drove home to be with my family over the holidays.

I relaxed with a few books. In one of them a man talked about his experiences in mission work all over the world, including the Middle East and Asia and Africa. All of a sudden I flipped a page, and he was in Northern Ireland.

I hadn't expected it, but I read the chapter anyway. He talked about the period called the Troubles, the shootings and bombings and hatred between Irish who wanted to remain connected to Britain and others who wanted to join the Republic of Ireland. He talked about things he had seen Christ do in response to the faith of a few people. I was inspired, as I had been by the talk in chapel months before. But then I closed the book, and that was that.

Before I got out of the chair, the strangest sensation went right through me. I felt compelled to go to Ireland. I protested, "Lord, I can't. The deadline has passed." But then I felt an even stronger urging from his Spirit, and in an instant all my objections were swept away. I was meant to go to Ireland, regardless of my fears. I was bewildered, delighted, and challenged all at the same time.

So I began to get out of the boat, and odd things happened. At Christmas dinner my mother said she didn't mind if I went anywhere in the world as a minister — as long as I never went to Northern Ireland. Back at school I felt some doubts about my book-reading conversion and went into a prayer room to agonize over the whole matter. When I walked out of the room, the student who was organizing the Irish mission trip — who happened to be Irish himself — was waiting to get into the prayer room himself.

I was astonished to see him. He said hello, and I blurted, "I've got to go to Ireland!" He said my eyes were wide as soccer balls. "All right," he responded, not sure what else to do, even though they weren't taking any more applications.

The waves came up, and the wind was against me. Some of the team members didn't want me to go. I needed a certain number of dollars by such and such a date, and while others had been gathering funds for months, I had only a few weeks. I needed to tell my mother about what I was intending to do. Would she be able to handle it or could it plunge her into a state of anxiety and fear?

The money came in, mostly from fellow students. The mission team bonded, and we grew to love one another. My mother grew proud of what I had decided to do. That summer I went to Ireland and wound up talking to people on their doorsteps, preaching gospel messages to crowds on market days, writing and acting out stories and dramas for children and teens, playing soccer with fifty players on a side and cow pies always underfoot like patches of ice. It was one of the most astonishing summers of my life, and it changed me completely—as good summers often can. The children we spoke with and listened to, the youth, the adults, the lives we blessed and the lives that blessed us, there was never another summer like it. I was walking where I had never walked before, and I kept walking, even in the wind and the waves.

For there were wind and waves, though not so much within the team as all around us—shootings, killings, kneecappings, teens being kicked to death by street gangs. When we spoke with the Irish, we did not focus on Protestant and Catholic, Loyalist or Republican, choosing one side or another; it was all about Jesus and about God's love for everyone. Even when we drove back up from our few weeks at Carlow in the South and got tangled in the traffic and smoke and shattered bodies of South Down's Warrenpoint Massacre—our Irish friends in Belfast frantic with the fear we had been caught in the blasts—it still had to be Jesus and forgiveness or else there was no message to give to Ireland.

That was August 27, 1979—Lord Mountbatten blown to pieces on his boat *Shadow V* at Mullaghmore in County Sligo in the South, a place we had driven past a few hours after it happened, and eighteen British soldiers dead in two bombs at Warrenpoint, just as we came over the border, dark smoke and confusion and army helicopters roaring over our heads. There are things you never forget when you climb out of the boat and walk where Jesus asks you to walk. Sometimes it is where the heartbreak and carnage is greatest. Northern Ireland has seen its civilians killed, its fathers and mothers and children, its police and its soldiers. And as you walk on those waters with Jesus, you see that he cares about all of them. It doesn't matter which side they're on.

Walking on water is not easy, and it is not common. Sometimes we need to be in our boats and crossing our lakes. Sometimes we've been out of our boats long enough and need to get back in them. Sometimes there are things to do on shore. But sometimes Jesus invites us to walk on water that is torn by wind and storm, and if we can find the faith to walk there with him, it changes us—and, one walk at a time, it changes the world we live in.

SIX

When your world caves in, you look for a place in which you do not have to think much and where you do not have to feel much, and sometimes, by the grace of God, it is a place familiar to you, a place in which old and pleasant rhythms can reassert themselves and, over time, bring a measure of healing.

For several of the disciples, it was the waters of the lake, fishing nets in hand. Their hero was dead—murdered—and the wonderful three-year upheaval in their lives was over. They went back to what they knew. Perhaps they even used the boat Jesus had told stories from, crossed the lake with, and calmed the storm in. "I'm going out to fish," Peter said, and that was that (John 21:3).

James and John joined him. So did Thomas and Nathanael and two other disciples. The sun was setting. They pushed the hull off from the beach and sailed into deeper waters. They fished under the moon and stars. They fished all night. They didn't catch anything, but maybe they didn't care. They just wanted to do something they understood, and the familiar rituals of playing with the sail and rudder and casting the nets probably felt good to them after experiencing an overload of life experiences that made no sense.

Jesus had done amazing things, said amazing things, made such an incredible difference in each of their lives. But the one who had raised others from the dead could not prevent himself from being killed. Peter, in particular, was not happy about his performance during the arrest and trial. "I don't know him; I don't know him"—that was all he could say, using foul language he thought he had left behind after the first dozen miracles he'd witnessed: "He began to call down curses on himself, and he swore to them, 'I don't know this man you're talking about'" (Mark 14:71).

He was ashamed of himself. Perhaps he hoped the rough feeling of rope, the snap of flapping sails and waves, and the sight of schools of fish could erase the pain in his heart. Yet what made it worse was somehow, in a way he and the others could not understand, Jesus had come back from the dead, at least that's what it looked like. Jesus had shown up in their room in Jerusalem without coming through the door. He'd spoken with them. They'd seen the wounds in his hands and feet and side—and it had stunned them. But when he wasn't around, the whole thing went back to making no sense. Was it a ghost of Jesus or an angel? How could it really be him? And after each visit Peter would lie awake while the others slept and think to himself, "He didn't mention my betrayal. He must know about it. When is he going to bring it up?" And he had no peace.

So he went to the lake that did make sense, and others went with him. Now he was pulling the net in with John at his shoulder grunting, but again it was empty.

"Why don't we row closer to shore?" suggested James.

Peter shrugged: *"Lama lo?"* Why not?

The sun was coming up, and the water was hammered

copper. Peter shivered and pulled his heavy cloak on. He squinted at the shore. Someone was standing there. Was it Andrew, his brother?

"Haverim!" Friends!

"What does he want?" asked Thomas grumpily.

"Who knows?" answered Nathanael.

"Haverim!"

"Who is it?" demanded Thomas.

"Who knows?" answered Nathanael.

"Do you have any fish?"

"Ah," grunted John, "he wants to buy some—that's what this is about."

"Well, we don't have any," growled James.

"You tell him," said John.

"No!" shouted James.

"The fish are on the right side of your boat! Throw your net out there! You'll get a catch!"

"What?" asked James.

"His voice carried well enough," said John. "You heard him."

"Cast our net on the right side of the boat? You can't be serious. What difference is that going to make?"

"What does it matter?" shrugged Peter. "Nothing else has worked. Maybe he's a genius. Maybe he's worked this part of the lake at dawn. Cast it over the right side."

James shook his head. "If you say so."

Peter yanked off his cloak so he could get a better throw. The cluster of them got the timing just right and flung the net over the side. Nothing happened.

"You see," smiled James.

"Wait a minute," said Thomas. "Something's going on."

James looked. "Haul up!" he shouted. "Haul up! The net is going to break!"

They all grabbed at the lines and pulled, but the net wouldn't budge.

"It's full. We can't move it," gasped James, straining.

John looked at the man on the shore. His eyes met Peter's. "It is the Lord."

Peter had known and not known the voice, but John's confirmation was all he needed. He did not stop to think. He threw on his cloak and dived into the copper water. Jerkily, his arms and legs not cooperating in his excitement, he swam for the beach. The others came after him in the boat, towing the net crammed with fish. When they came ashore, and Peter hauled himself out of the lake, they all saw the same thing—a fire of coals with some fish already on it and several loaves of bread.

"Bring some of the fresh fish you just caught," said the man squatting by the fire. "We'll roast them."

Peter helped drag the net onto the land and brought some of the large fish over to the fire. The man took them and placed them carefully on the heat. "*Toda raba*," he said. Thank you.

"Who is it?" whispered Nathanael.

"You know who it is," hissed Thomas.

After a few minutes of turning the bread and fish, the man called them over. "Come and have breakfast!"

They came and sat in a circle. The man picked the bread up from the fire and passed it around. He did the same with the roasted fish. His movements reminded them of another time by this same lake years before when a man had handed out bread and fish.

Nathanael nodded. "It *is* him."

Slowly they began to unbend and talk while they ate. Everything tasted very good. Even the water seemed to have a special bite to it. And they started to talk with him too — the man, Jesus. It really was Jesus. "Had the night felt long?" he asked them. "How do you feel being back at the lake? How is the food? Do you want anymore to eat?"

When they were done, Jesus turned to Peter and gently asked him three times if Peter loved him. Three times Peter said yes, though by the third time he was beginning to feel hurt. Yet it was Peter's restoration from the deeper hurt of the three betrayals. Three times Jesus asked him to shepherd and feed his lambs and sheep, to be a leader. Then he told him that one day, because of his love for Jesus and his people, enemies would come for Peter and take his life, but it would be a death of honor that would open eyes to God's wonder and glory.

And though Jesus did not say it that day by the lake, James would be the first to die, beheaded. John, his brother, would be exiled to the island of Patmos. Thomas, so the story went, would die taking the gospel to India. They had known so much life by the shores of the lake, and they would take that life to others who lived by many other shores. And what more incredible tale to tell about Jesus than that after he rose from the dead, he met them at their lake, helped them catch a net full of fish, and then cooked breakfast for them—using some of those same fish—as if his resurrection from the grave was the most natural and normal thing in the world.

And maybe it is.

SEVEN

Water played a huge role in Jesus' life.

His first miracle was turning the water at the wedding feast in Cana into wine (John 2:1 – 11).

He applied his own spit to a man's tongue to give the man his voice back (Mark 7:33 – 35).

He spoke to a Samaritan woman at Jacob's ancient well, asked her for a drink, and then told her he could offer her something better than well water: "Everyone who drinks this water will be thirsty again, but those who drink the water I give them will never thirst. Indeed, the water I give them will become in them a spring of water welling up to eternal life" (John 4:13 – 14 TNIV).

During the Feast of Tabernacles, he once declared loudly, "Let anyone who is thirsty come to me and drink. Whoever believes in me, as Scripture has said, rivers of living water will flow from within them" (John 7:37 – 38 TNIV).

He made mud with his spit, placed the mud on a blind man's eyes, and told him to wash in the pool of Siloam — and the man's eyesight was restored (John 9:1 – 11).

At Passover, before his arrest and crucifixion, he washed the feet of his disciples (John 13:1 – 17).

On the cross, he cried out that he was thirsty — but on the

sponge that came to his lips was not water but wine vinegar (John 19:28–30).

When a Roman soldier thrust a spear into his side after his death, there was a gush of blood and water (John 19:34).

The one who said, "Let anyone who is thirsty come to me and drink," was also the one who said, "I thirst." The one who told the woman at the well he could offer living water that would become a spring of eternal life inside her was also the one who oozed water and blood at his death. The sacrifice Jesus made on the cross was very great, and it seemed to undo the person he really was. The wonderful thing is this: the very sacrifice that turned him from living water into a man dying of thirst was the very sacrifice that made his living water available to all.

There are other water stories. Some of the most moving involve the water that flows from our eyes. Jesus shed tears at the grave of his friend Lazarus. He also shed tears over Jerusalem: "If you, even you, had only known on this day what would bring you peace—but now it is hidden from your eyes" (Luke 19:42). A woman cried at Jesus' feet and wiped them with her long hair. Jesus said, "Her many sins have been forgiven—as her great love has shown" (Luke 7:47 TNIV).

Water in Jesus' life is connected to cleansing and healing, to commitment and renewal and life. His baptism is commitment to God the Father and his mission; ours is commitment to Christ and the renewal of our lives. His thirst on the cross is commitment to our salvation; to us it is real life that cannot end. Washing the disciples' feet is love for and commitment to his followers; for them it is cleansing. Everything Jesus does with water is a commitment to the Father and to us.

So many beautiful things happened around the lake or on it that it seems right for the gospel of John, the final gospel, to end there on its shores — as if to say, this place was very special to Jesus and his disciples. And so it is fitting he went there after he rose from the dead, fitting we should be left with a final glorious impression of Jesus and his lake and his miracles, fitting he should walk by its waters once more and show us his love and unwavering commitment before he left the earth, fitting we should linger there and look at the water and waves and remember all he was and all he still is.

TIDES

The afternoon was a mix of sun and clouds. The water was ruffled by a few waves. The temperature was not too cool, not too hot, perfect for rowing. So my wife and I hauled out the yellow boat and put the oars in their locks and got at it.

We did not move out into the open sea. The cove was enough. It was large, fringed by trees and beach and beautiful homes, dotted with powerboats and sailing ships at their moorings. Plenty of places to go, lots of things to see. We took turns at the oars and zigzagged across the water from beach to jetty to rocky headland.

My wife and I enjoyed the rowing, but neither of us was in a very good mood. It's kind of surprising we decided to go out in the boat at all—no one usually wants to exert themselves if they're feeling low. I guess we both had the idea we had to do something to pull ourselves out of the hole—and maybe the sea air would help.

A lot of things had piled up in our hearts—struggles at our church, struggles with her work, struggles with finances, with relationships, with trying to figure out why God seemed to be answering some prayers but not the ones that mattered most to us. We rowed and rowed. Sometimes the wind was with us, sometimes against us.

We talked, first about the things that hurt us, then about

the things that angered us, then about the things that puzzled us. Then, somehow or other, we started talking about the good things that had happened long, long ago.

"Do you remember when God did this? Do you remember when God did that?" There was the time he answered those prayers, and we couldn't believe it. The time that woman came to Christ. The time those sisters were baptized together. The time no one could take Communion without weeping. The morning we never stopped the worship team, and so the whole church sang until past noon.

It is an ancient practice, of course. In Scripture we see again and again how people remind one another of what God did in the past to give themselves strength to face both the present and the future. What God did before he can do again. It must be so. Didn't he say he would be with us "even unto the end of the world"? (Matthew 28:20 KJV).

Human nature tends to grip the bad experiences, the ones that have really wounded us, and let the good experiences go. They are still in the background, of course, those good memories, and we recall them from time to time, but the hurts that still hurt and the disappointments that still disappoint take up most of our energy and our thoughts. If we can open the door just a crack and let some good mingle with the bad, it can refresh our spirits—even, over time, help heal our spiritual cuts and abrasions and burns. But we do not do it often enough.

The Red Sea, the rivers of Babylon, the desert streams that course through the badlands, the Jordan, and the lake in Galilee —all these are trips the soul can take, water journeys that remind us of how God rescues, comforts, saves, heals, renews, and raises from the dead. These waters are meant to bring close to us God's stories of how he has always worked with and blessed his people — and also to bring back into our hearts and minds God's stories of how he has always worked with us and blessed our lives, even when we thought all was lost. The Bible stories are not just old stories; they are *our* stories. And each generation of believers lives them out again and again until the end of time. God is always faithful and always there, and the seas part, the deserts bloom, and the storms are calmed.

By the time the two of us had finished our row, the sun was dropping and the stars were on their way. Our hearts brimmed with the crimson, bronze, and emerald of the skies. We were full of color and light. God had filled us; our memories had filled us. Words of faith that recalled the many times God had met us in our need — times he carried us and would not let us go — filled us. And we laughed and knew his peace once again.

> *When the LORD restored the fortunes of Zion,*
> *we were like those who dreamed.*
> *Our mouths were filled with laughter,*
> *our tongues with songs of joy.*
> *Then it was said among the nations,*
> *"The LORD has done great things for them."*
> *The LORD has done great things for us,*
> *and we are filled with joy*
>
> Psalm 126:1 – 3 TNIV

ACKNOWLEDGMENTS

This book goes out with gratitude to the rugged wordsmith of intense Montana sky and mountains, Eugene Peterson —Anam Cara, soul friend—and to my agent, Les Stobbe, to my editorial team at HarperCollins and Zondervan of Andy Meisenheimer and Dirk Buursma, as well as to Tom Dean in marketing. Thanks for all your support and hard work. Thanks to my wife, Linda, another wonderful Anam Cara; my son, Micah; and my daughter, Micaela. Your warmth and love mean all the world to me. Thanks to the many brothers and sisters in Christ in many different countries who have always believed in my writing and to the many churches where I have served whose stories and struggles became part of my own pilgrimage in Jesus, a pilgrimage reflected in these pages. Thanks especially to Heartland Community Church, 1998-2010, who always wanted me to write and always gave me the space, prayers, and encouragement to do so. Thanks also to the seekers and wonderers who often cross my path or walk with me a while with their questions and their quest for truth. Thanks, Mark, for pushing me, and thanks, James, for challenging me to write not simply for the few but the many. And, once again and always, I thank God.

Rooted

Reflections on the Gardens in Scripture

Murray Andrew Pura

Brimming with beauty and full of metaphors in the life of Christ, gardens are symbolic places of birth, death, and resurrection.

Respected author, pastor, and gardener Murray Andrew Pura revisits the five major gardens of the Bible and explores the spiritual meanings they symbolize. From creation to Revelation, readers will glean new insights into leading a fulfilling Christian life.

Each of the five major gardens has something to say to Christians today:

> The garden of Eden, and our fall from innocence
> En Gedi, and God's love for us
> Gethsemane, and suffering
> The Garden Tomb, and the hope of resurrection
> Second Eden, and a new world breaking through

As Pura unearths fresh insight about the deeper symbolism rooted in each garden, readers are nourished by a renewed understanding of their role in God's growing kingdom.

Hardcover, Printed: 978-0-310-31837-8

Share Your Thoughts

With the Author: Your comments will be forwarded to the author when you send them to *zauthor@zondervan.com*.

With Zondervan: Submit your review of this book by writing to *zreview@zondervan.com*.

Free Online Resources at
www.zondervan.com

Zondervan AuthorTracker: Be notified whenever your favorite authors publish new books, go on tour, or post an update about what's happening in their lives at www.zondervan.com/authortracker.

Daily Bible Verses and Devotions: Enrich your life with daily Bible verses or devotions that help you start every morning focused on God. Visit www.zondervan.com/newsletters.

Free Email Publications: Sign up for newsletters on Christian living, academic resources, church ministry, fiction, children's resources, and more. Visit www.zondervan.com/newsletters.

Zondervan Bible Search: Find and compare Bible passages in a variety of translations at www.zondervanbiblesearch.com.

Other Benefits: Register yourself to receive online benefits like coupons and special offers, or to participate in research.

ZONDERVAN®

ZONDERVAN.com/
AUTHORTRACKER
follow your favorite authors